PREPARING
for
RETIREMENT

LARRY BURKETT

PREPARING *for* RETIREMENT

MOODY PRESS

CHICAGO

Printed on recycled paper stock

This book is dedicated to our Lord, Jesus Christ, who promises us the only sure retirement plan.

"But seek first His kingdom and His righteousness, and all these things shall be added to you. Therefore do not be anxious for tomorrow; for tomorrow will care for itself. Each day has enough trouble of its own."

(Matthew 6: 33-34).

Contents

Introduction

Retirement, usually at 62 to 65, is something that most us of have come to accept as an attainable goal after our working careers. In fact, since the advent of Social Security in the thirties, it has become an assumed right.

In many ways the concept of retirement was good for the economy in the past since it freed positions for younger workers to fill. But the dynamics of the American work force have been altered greatly during the last two decades. Abortions and birth control have decimated the generation that will be entering the market place in the twenty-first century.

From 1946 to 1964 approximately seventy million baby boomers were born—thirty million more than would be the norm for our society. As a result, according to statistics from the U.S. Census Bureau, Americans ages 55 to 74 will increase from approximately forty million in 1989 to over seventy million by the year 2010—just when the middle age population is in its most rapid decline.

In addition, health care and extended life cycles have driven up the cost of retirement. Simply put, people live longer, collect more benefits, and utilize more expensive life support systems. The demand for more taxes to support the retirees places ever-increasing burdens on those who have not yet attained their "golden years." Consequently, the liabilities to society of retirement now far outweigh the assets.

When the idea of old age pensions was first proposed in 1934, the average life expectancy of a man was approximately 63. For the designers of Social Security, as well as insurance company annuitants, providing retirement benefits that started at 65 was an economically sound idea. Theoretically, the vast majority of the participants would never live to use their benefits. But because of better health care, fewer work hours, and generally better health habits, the average man's life expectancy today is about 73. (Women generally have a life expectancy of two to three years more than men, although the difference tends to narrow after the age of 70.)

I believe the keys to good planning for the future are found in the timeless wisdom of God's Word. Therefore, the great majority of financial decisions can be made on the basis of God's principles.

So here we are with a retirement concept that was designed to make a worker's "twilight years" more comfortable (Social Security was designed only as a supplement to retirement) in a generation in which the average worker recovers his or her total contributions to the system in five years or less. It is a virtual certainty in the next century that those living on Social Security alone will be relegated to the impoverished class unless some very prudent planning is done before approaching retirement.

As you will learn in this book, there are some very sobering economic problems facing our nation in the twenty-first century that will very likely force the vast majority of retirees back into the work place. Those who are not aware and prepared may end up a part of the homeless explosion in our cities. By no means do I believe this is inevitable. With good financial planning and God's help, the elderly can lead productive and comfortable lives well into their eighties and nineties. But the one phrase we will all have to eliminate from our vocabulary in the next decade is: That can't happen here!

Most of the nation's major financial magazines have carried numerous articles on the failure of insurance companies, banks, and major pension plans during the late eighties and early nineties. Any current or future retiree would do well to heed the signs of economic decay in our society and not get trapped by a "prosperity forever" mentality. However, it would be equally shortsighted to orient all of your planning toward a "calamity" mind set.

I believe the keys to good planning for the future are found in the timeless wisdom of God's Word. Therefore, the great majority of financial decisions can be made on the basis of God's principles.

I have spent the last twenty years of my life studying the biblical principles for money management and applying them in my own life. If you will commit to doing likewise, you will discover a biblical absolute: You can rely on God's wisdom, regardless of the economy.

Allow me to use an example. In our generation a great deal of attention is focused on generating quick profits. And, in

fact, many people have been able to do so by high-risk speculation in a variety of "investments" from real estate to stocks. But
it has been my observation that very few speculators are able to
keep what they make. More often than not the same get-rich-
quick mentality, which makes money for speculators originally,
later causes them to take even greater risks; eventually they
lose most of what they make.

This mentality is particularly disastrous at an older age
when the losses cannot be recouped. Speculation, in and of
itself, is not necessarily wrong but, when taken to extremes, it
becomes a get-rich-quick mentality. The wisdom of Solomon
still holds true today: *"A man with an evil eye hastens after
wealth, and does not know that want will come upon him"*
(Proverbs 28:22). Before launching into a discussion on retirement, I want to explain why I wrote this book and what you
should expect to gain from reading it.

This book is not meant to be merely an investment guide
for retirees (or those approaching retirement), but rather a
comprehensive handbook for retirees, present and future. To
be sure, if you fail to plan financially, retirement can be a frus-
trating and fearful time. But the best financial planning in the
world done in the nineties may be worthless in the twenty-first
century if you don't take into account future health care costs,
inflation, the economy, taxes, and so on. Therefore, I will try to
help you think through each of these areas and make the best
decisions possible as you approach retirement age. But, more
important, it is my desire that you understand how to evaluate
future changes for yourself and adjust accordingly.

There is an old cliché: *Information without application
leads to frustration.* This is usually the case with the families I
have counseled who attended seminars, read books, and even
sought good counsel, but did nothing as a result of what they
learned. More often than not, the reason people do nothing is
because they hear so many conflicting viewpoints they become
paralyzed by confusion. At some point you must decide to take
the plunge and make a decision. In other words, do something!

My advice and observations certainly are not infallible; all
too often the opposite is true. But if you will weigh what you
read against God's principles found in the Bible, you'll find that

I never purposely give advice contrary to that in God's Word. I have spent the last twenty years of my life studying the biblical principles for money management and applying them in my own life. If you will commit to doing likewise, you will discover a biblical absolute: You can rely on God's wisdom, regardless of the economy.

As I try to evaluate what the economy of the twenty-first century will be like, it's almost impossible to comprehend the changes that will take place. There will be as many economic changes from the twentieth to the twenty-first century as there were technological changes from the nineteenth to the twentieth centuries.

My father lived to see the transition from horse-drawn carriages to jet planes. I have seen the transition from vacuum tube radios that weighed thirty pounds to television sets that can be carried in a shirt pocket. Early in the next century we will see the end of all currency in exchange for a worldwide cash-less economy. If the present trend prevails, we will see people living longer, but with steadily declining lifestyles. As America slips from an industrial to a service-oriented economy, there will be fewer jobs at lower salaries; production will migrate to the developing countries that have cheaper labor bases and fewer regulations.

My plan in this book is to present a balanced perspective of what you can expect well into the next century and help you to plan accordingly.

Sometime before the end of this century and the beginning of the next, it seems very likely that we will have a major economic depression, caused by our massive accumulation of debt. If, as I believe, this depression is coupled with runaway inflation caused by our government printing money to cover its deficits, then all the rules for modern-day economics will be rewritten. As I read through the statistics on our economy, and our nation as a whole, my thoughts often go back to 1958—my senior year in high school. Somewhere between my junior and senior year, my interest in history was sparked—a passion that continues even today. I remember that I was reading through a copy of *The Rise and Fall of the Roman Empire* when I thought to myself, *How could those people have been so stupid that they ignored the indicators all around them? Their indulgences finally led to the collapse of their economy and ultimately their civilization.* Well, here we are today, repeating their mistakes on a scale beyond their wildest imaginations.

In reality, the economic decline of America is merely tracking our moral and social decline—all of which can be traced to a single root cause: a denial of God. Any nation that denies the existence of God will ultimately ignore the principles taught in God's Word. When that happens the slide into mediocrity is a virtual certainty. As the Apostle Paul said in Romans 1:28, *"And just as they did not see fit to acknowledge God any longer, God gave them over to a depraved mind, to do those things which are not proper."*

Anyone who attempts to do any realistic retirement planning without taking into account the signs of a rapidly changing economy is being very nearsighted. But, as I said earlier, you cannot do all of your planning based on a "crisis" mentality either. To do so will either drive you into a shell, in which case you'll bury all your assets in the backyard, or it will tempt you to risk everything in get-rich-quick schemes, as you try to "beat the system."

My plan in this book is to present a balanced perspective of what you can expect well into the next century and help you to plan accordingly. For some, my approach may be too conservative—especially those who look (and even hope) for an economic apocalypse.

If an apocalypse does indeed occur, the best financial planning most of us could do would be inadequate. Only the very wealthy or the very poor maintain their relative positions in an economic collapse. I don't expect the entire economy to fail, although a major economic "adjustment" seems inevitable at some point in the future.

Understand that even during the Great Depression in the thirties only 24 percent of American workers were unemployed, and 30 percent of the businesses failed. It is unlikely that the next depression would exceed the last. But if your money is invested in a failed company, the depth and breadth of the problem is pretty much irrelevant. The key to good planning is in being among the surviving 70 percent.

*T*his book is meant to be a handbook for the plethora of decisions you must make, such as whether to buy more life insurance, purchase nursing home insurance, use a living trust, or prepay funeral expenses. The critical decisions you will make between now and the year 2000 are important. But, again I emphasize that the best any person can do is give you advice. Only God can give true wisdom.

I realize that some readers will feel that I present too pessimistic a view of the future. After *The Coming Economic Earthquake* (Moody Press) was published in 1991, I was severely criticized in articles and reviews written by investment salespeople. Reading between the lines I could see what was happening; many of their clients were coming in and telling them, "I read this book *(The Coming Economic Earthquake)* and I believe it. I think I'll stop my investments for a couple of years while I pay off my debts." Consequently, some investment advisors attacked the book for being too radical.

Personally I don't see a volatile economy as being a negative for financial advisors. In reality, just the opposite should be true. Almost anyone can prosper in a stable, secure economy if they earn enough and save a reasonable percentage of it. But economic survival during a depression and/or inflation requires good counsel and quick reflexes. Good investment advisors can help their clients to diversify as a hedge against both situations.

To plan only for a growing, non-inflationary economy over the next ten years or so, I believe, is very imprudent. If I'm wrong about a depression followed by hyperinflation, the worst that can happen is you'll end up with a diversified retirement portfolio. But if I'm right, and you do nothing to prepare, you can end up on welfare.

The economic scenario I will presume is that both events —depression and inflation—will occur sometime before the end of this decade in rapid succession. This will primarily affect the investment side of retirement planning. Most other decisions will not change radically, irrespective of the economy.

Keep in mind that this book is not an investment guide for those planning retirement. I covered that topic in the book *Investing for the Future* (Victor Books). This book is meant to be a handbook for the plethora of decisions you must make, such as whether to buy more life insurance, purchase nursing home insurance, use a living trust, or prepay funeral expenses. The critical decisions you will make between now and the year 2000 are important. But, again I emphasize that the best any person can do is give you advice. Only God can give true *wisdom*.

I will begin this book with a reminder from Solomon—the world's wisest man: *"How blessed is the man who finds wisdom, and the man who gains understanding. For its profit is better than the profit of silver, and its gain than fine gold"* (Proverbs 3:13-15).

*I*s retirement itself a biblical principle God established for His people? Since there is so little Scripture dealing with this subject, it would seem logical to make one of two assumptions: Either God forgot to discuss the subject of retirement, or it is not a part of His plan for us. I discovered long ago that God doesn't forget anything; therefore it has to be that our whole perspective of retirement is out of balance.

CHAPTER ONE

The Facts About Retirement

According to the Social Security Advisory Council's annual report for 1991, retirement in America is due for some drastic changes by the end of this century. The report points to a shrinking work force and expanding retirement sector as the single greatest problem facing future retirees. The report looked at three future scenarios of income and payments through the Social Security system over the next twenty-five years or so. The present "pay-as-you-go" plan simply won't work, unless workers in the next decade are willing to fork over 40 to 50 percent of their wages to retirees.

When the Old Age Benefit system began in the mid-1930s, there were approximately fourteen contributors for every potential retiree. By 1990 that figure had declined to approximately four workers for every retiree, and by 2010 it is estimated (under the best scenario) to decline to less than a three-to-one ratio. This is due to a number of factors that we will discuss, but suffice it to say that three working taxpayers (especially lower-income taxpayers) cannot adequately support one retiree in any degree of comfort.

Essentially this means that either the majority of Americans must plan for and fund their *own* retirement, which is highly unlikely given the current "spend-as-you-go" mentality, or plan to keep on working. In reality the best alternative probably lies somewhere in between.

Before discussing the details of what decisions must be made to plan for a reasonably comfortable retirement, I would first like to discuss some basic biblical principles that will help to define retirement.

Anyone who has accepted Jesus Christ as Savior has made the decision to live his or her life according to God's directions (to the highest degree possible). In order to do that, a Christian must first learn God's basic principles. These are found in the Bible—God's manual for living.

It is my firm conviction that any advice (regardless of who gives it) that cannot be validated on the basis of God's Word is just an opinion. We all have opinions; some opinions are better than others, depending on the person's level of expertise.

*P*ersonally, I believe it is best
to start a retirement program
at about the age of 40, and
only after paying off *all* loans,
including your home mortgage.

For instance, if you want my opinion on which car to buy, I can identify those that get the best gas mileage, require the lowest rate of repairs, and have the highest average resale value. All of these factors are verifiable statistically.

But the decision about which is *the* best car is still just my opinion because, as near as I can tell, God has not detailed in His Word the best car to buy. And since only the Lord can know if you would get a lemon, all I can do is make an educated guess. Also, I would probably recommend that you buy a red car since red cars usually have a better resale value, but you might not like red cars, so you would be dissatisfied.

If the subject under discussion changes to a topic like brain surgery, my best opinion becomes woefully inadequate. A skilled neurosurgeon would be the best source of advice on that topic. However, a visit to any three neurologists will verify that each has a slightly different perspective on what the right course of action should be.

The same principle can be applied to financial advisors, attorneys, accountants, or auto mechanics. If you're totally dependent on someone else's counsel, you can be certain you'll get some bad advice from time to time.

The majority of Americans are constantly inundated with conflicting advice, especially on the topic of retirement. One advisor says to start investing for retirement at a very young age since the money will compound for a longer period of time. Time is a very important factor when compounding is considered. Obviously the longer the money is compounded, the larger it grows. So, why not start your retirement program at age 25? Because it's been my observation that the temptation to take that money out and spend it on indulgences is too great for many people to resist.

Personally, I believe it is best to start a retirement program at about the age of 40, and *only* after paying off *all* loans, including your home mortgage.

So, who should you listen to? your financial advisor? or me? The answer is: neither of us—totally. The best we can do is present the various alternatives as we see them from our limited perspective. The primary counsel you should seek is the Lord's. Only He knows if you will live long enough to accomplish your goals, or if your investments will still be around when you need the money.

From my perspective as a family financial counselor, I have seen a lot of good and bad (mostly bad) financial decisions. I think of all the people I have known who invested in American Motors, Eastern Airlines, Pan American—even the

PTL club; their investments are gone, but most of their debts linger on. Based on this observation (with rare exception), I advise people to pay off their debts first since paying off debt is the one *sure* investment available.

But on the other side are those who invested in high-growth companies like IBM and Microsoft and saw their money grow by 1,000 percent. Well, that's why you should seek the *Lord's* counsel. God's Word teaches that debt should not be the norm for His people. Although the Bible doesn't prohibit borrowing, it does establish some practical guidelines, one of which is: Don't stay in debt long-term. Biblically, the longest debt period for God's people was seven years, or less. That's why I teach the principle of paying off debt before starting a retirement plan.

Most Christians *say* they want God's counsel in their financial decisions. But the majority, if they were totally honest, would admit that they aren't totally committed to following His counsel except in a crisis. And even then they're not really sure they can recognize God's counsel from among the jangle of advice they try to sort through.

By definition, all true Christians believe in the existence of Jesus Christ. Christians also believe that Jesus died for their redemption and He intercedes on their behalf with His Father in heaven. Christians believe that when they die they will go to be with the Lord and will be able to talk with Him. Unfortunately, what most don't believe is that such a dialogue is possible in this life and on this earth.

If Christians really believed it was possible to ask questions of Jesus and receive specific answers in response, they would be living different lifestyles and planning a lot differently (including retirement). I say that not as an indictment against other Christians; I include myself in that same category.

Even when we strive to serve the Lord, the society around us molds us into its image. As a result, it becomes increasingly difficult to separate God's voice from the cacophony of sounds around us. This is due, in large part, to the fact that we have difficulty attuning our minds to God's "frequency."

Allow me to use an example. Not long ago, while flying from Atlanta to Dallas, I found a magazine on psychiatry in the seat pocket in front of me. Since I am prone to read whatever literature I can find (to distract me while flying), I leafed through this magazine, expecting to find nothing of interest. Instead, I discovered a research article on something called RAS (reticular articulation syndrome). Although I was unfamiliar with the terminology, I found that I was totally familiar with the concept. RAS, the writer explained, is the ability to focus one's mind on areas of interest so that all other distractions are virtually eliminated from consciousness.

For instance, RAS is the reason that a mother can hear her child crying in a room of twenty screaming children; she has assimilated her child's voice into her retention pattern. In other words, she has prioritized her mind to distinguish her child's voice from among many others.

*R*etirement, as we know it, is so new that most current retirees can still remember when practically no one retired. In my grandfather's generation certainly few, if any, ordinary citizens would have seriously considered that they could stop working and play golf at 65 or so.

We all do this in one way or another on a daily basis. I love old cars, and one of my favorite hobbies is restoring these relics of the past, which otherwise would go to the junk heaps. I can usually detect the outline of an early model car even if it's covered with vines and other undergrowth. I can assure you though that my wife, Judy, does not share this passion, even though she tolerates having our garage used as a rescue center for derelict cars. She is more into antiques—like furniture and other uninteresting (to me) stuff.

One summer when we were traveling to North Carolina to visit my mother, I spotted several old cars well back off of the road. Knowing that I had been less than patient some miles back when Judy had wanted to stop and look in an antique store, I didn't even suggest that we stop and look at the cars. Imagine my surprise when she asked, "Did you see that?"

"Sure," I replied."Would you mind if we go back and take a look?"

She said "Okay" so enthusiastically that I thought I just might have been successful in convincing her that old cars are more important than old furniture. I wheeled the car around and parked as near as I could to the old cars. But when I started to get out she asked,"Why are we stopping here?"

I replied somewhat cautiously,"Because this is where the cars are."

"But I wanted to go there," she said as she pointed to an antique store a little farther down on the other side of the road. She hadn't even noticed the cars I had spotted, and I certainly didn't notice the antique store. Why? Because of our different RAS.

The same basic principle is true today in Christianity. Most of us have our RAS attuned to the world around us and, consequently, we miss the road signs God puts in our paths. God is speaking, but we're on different frequencies. The way we get back onto His wavelength is by reconfirming our vows to follow His path—no matter what the world around us is doing. That is fundamental if we are to settle this issue of retirement planning. The question is: Are you willing to make your decisions according to God's Word, even when it conflicts with all the counsel around you?

Is Retirement Scriptural?

I am convinced that retirement, as we know it in our generation, is not scriptural. I'm not implying that someone who retires at age 62 or 65 is living in sin. There are some instances where retirement is a part of God's plan for a particular individual. But the basic concept of idling the majority of people at such an early age is a modern innovation, *not* a biblical principle.

There is actually only one direct reference to retirement in the *Bible:"This is what applies to the Levites: from twenty-five years old and upward they shall enter to perform service in the work of the tent of meeting. But at the age of fifty years they shall retire from service in the work and not work any more"* (Numbers 8:24-25).

*F*or our present system of retirement to function, two essential elements are required: first, a large class of workers who make sufficient incomes to save a sizeable portion for the future; and second, most of these workers must be so dissatisfied with their jobs that they're willing to quit at an early age.

Exactly why God directed that the priests should retire at 50 is not known. It is possible that they assisted in other functions but could not perform the ceremonies themselves. So if you're a Levite priest, according to God's Word your retirement decisions have been made. If you're not, read on.

Retirement, as we know it, is so new that most current retirees can still remember when practically no one retired. In my grandfather's generation certainly few, if any, ordinary citizens would have seriously considered that they could stop working and play golf at 65 or so.

In the first place, few Americans made enough money to be able to retire to the golf course. And those who did were so committed to their careers that they had little interest in retirement.

For our present system of retirement to function, two essential elements are required: first, a large class of workers who make sufficient incomes to save a sizeable portion for the future; and second, most of these workers must be so dissatisfied with their jobs that they're willing to quit at an early age.

Such a combination was found in two groups of workers during the fifties: union members and federal employees. As the labor unions grew in number and strength during the high employment period after World War II, their collective bargaining eventually took in long-term benefits, such as retirement. Companies were more than willing to negotiate for deferred benefits in lieu of current wage increases.

For the first time, retirement became an attainable goal for blue collar workers. The impact this idea was to have on American society was incalculable at that time. It would eventually give rise to a multi-billion dollar investment industry in the sixties, and would doom the Social Security system to failure as the majority of workers over sixty decided they *could* retire.

Once the retirement "bandwagon" got rolling, millions of additional people joined it. Eventually American workers became convinced that retirement is a basic "right." During the sixties and seventies laws were passed *requiring* workers to retire by age 65. With more and more younger workers coming into the work force, retirement became a logical way to free up jobs. As I said earlier, several factors now have made that same notion illogical—not the least of which is the lack of gainfully employed people to support the Social Security system.

Workers who planned to retire in the sixties, including my father (born in 1902), developed their retirement plans around Social Security and a modest company pension that would allow them a reasonably comfortable lifestyle. They had the best of all benefits: a growing economy, a growing labor force, low interest rates, and low inflation.

SOCIAL IN-SECURITY

Only three decades earlier, the Great Depression of the thirties had ended any thought of retirement for the average American worker of that day. Instead, for nearly ten years the emphasis for most Americans shifted to basic survival. At the outset of the Great Depression in the early thirties, millions of hard-working older Americans had been wiped out financially by the collapsing economy. Those beyond the age of 50 were often unemployable and yet, outside of finding whatever work they could, they had no means of living. The New Deal established the Old Age Pension Plan, now known as Social Security, as a means to bridge the gap for these workers.

The Roosevelt administration never intended that Social Security would be used as anything but an old age *supplement.* Social Security remained a supplemental income plan until after World War II, when politicians, vying for public favor, began to expand the system to match benefits in the private sector, including workers' disability, survivors' benefits, and more extensive retirement benefits.

Based on much of the material I have read from that era, it's quite possible the enhancement of the Social Security system was motivated by guilt over an ever-expanding federal retirement system. In an economy with nearly full employment, low-cost credit, and worldwide exports, little thought was given to the future costs of funding such a massive system.

By the late sixties, most Americans viewed retirement as a foregone conclusion. At age 65, you retire. In the seventies, the average retirement age had dropped to 62. Unfortunately the assumptions upon which most Americans based their hopes for retirement in the fifties and sixties changed drastically in the seventies and eighties, including Social Security.

But I'm getting ahead of myself. The basic issue I am addressing here is not the Social Security system; nor is it whether individuals can save enough to stop work at 62 and live comfortably. The real issue is: Is retirement itself a biblical principle God established for His people?

Since there is so little Scripture dealing with this subject, it would seem logical to make one of two assumptions: Either God forgot to discuss the subject of retirement, or it is not a part of His plan for us. I discovered long ago that God doesn't forget anything; therefore it has to be that our whole perspective of retirement is out of balance.

Having concluded that retirement (as we know it) is not scriptural, I would like to clarify what I mean. Although retirement is not biblical, it cannot be placed in the same category as objective sins—adultery, lying, stealing. These are expressly prohibited by God.

Retirement is not *prohibited,* it simply is not discussed to any degree. Therefore it is little more than an innovative way for modern society to escape the drudgery of work-place boredom. For some people it is a way to extend their useful years by seeking out new careers, supplemented by a retirement income. And for some, retirement is necessitated for health reasons. But, in general, retirement is not biblically endorsed.

Statistics indicate that retirement probably will not be possible for most Americans beyond the end of this century which, at the time of this writing, is less than ten years away. There simply will not be enough active workers to support all the retirees.

If God's plan for most of us is not retirement, then what is it?

Any logical observer would agree that the vast majority of people who live beyond the age of 70 are not capable of doing the same amount or level of work they were at ages 30, 40, 50, or even 60. The aging process lowers physical stamina, reflexes, and senses (although not necessarily mental faculties).

Often that's true even at a younger age. Just look at professional athletes. Few professional football players are gainfully employed as active athletes beyond the age of 35; none are beyond the age of 50. But since they're not employable as professional athletes, should they automatically conclude that their working careers are over? Hardly so. I know many ex–professional athletes who have started successful careers after retiring from their sports. Frank Gifford, Roger Staubach, Terry Bradshaw, and Fran Tarkenton are just a few. Some, like Jack

Kemp, have attained recognition in career fields totally removed from their athletic careers.

The point is, just because they can no longer do what they had been doing doesn't mean they can't do something! The same principle holds true for the rest of us. We may not be able to do the same things at 70 or 80 that we could do at 30 or 40, but we can do something useful and meaningful.

Some good friends, Walt and Ralph Meloon, are walking examples of this truth. For many years Walt and Ralph ran the Correct Craft boat company in Orlando, Florida. Now well into their seventies, both men have turned the day-to-day operations of Correct Craft over to their children. But Walt and Ralph have not settled down into their rocking chairs; nor do they spend their days on the golf courses of Florida. They're some of the most active men I know. Often when one or the other is passing through our area he'll stop over to have lunch. Usually they are traveling around the country visiting some of the Correct Craft distributors as ambassadors for the company.

A few years ago the Meloons started a ministry to help business people who are in financial distress and, often, in imminent danger of bankruptcy. They sponsor weekend sessions, called Turn-Around Weekends, where couples can come for advice and counsel. At these sessions both Walt and Ralph spend endless hours counseling with hurting people and sharing their own experiences about when Correct Craft was forced into bankruptcy during the early fifties.

Age has most certainly been a limiting factor for these two men of God, but they have simply found a way to be useful within these limitations. Christian history is full of examples of those who knew the biblical truth about retirement: It begins in eternity.

Remember: God uniquely created each of us, including our endurance and durability and, as a result, not everyone will have the same ability to work at the various stages of life. Consequently, there will be varying degrees of retirement for all of us. The degree to which we slow down is not the fundamental issue here; ceasing all productive activity is.

Statistics indicate that retirement probably will not be possible for most Americans beyond the end of this century which, at the time of this writing, is less than ten years away. There simply will not be enough active workers to support all the retirees.

*G*od has provided a plan for His people to rest and recover during their working lives. As best I can determine, God has not prescribed a time when we should retire. We have arbitrarily decided that at age 62, 65, or some later period, our active working careers should stop.

This leads to some pretty sobering conclusions: Either the majority of workers will continue to stay gainfully employed or society will find a convenient way to lower the costs of maintaining the non-productive ones. If you think euthanasia never can happen in America, just consider what those in their twenties and thirties are now doing to their unwanted offspring. This is the generation that will be in control of our country in the next century.

SABBATICALS

God in His infinite wisdom knew that His creation would need rest and relaxation. The method He chose to provide that rest and relaxation is called a sabbatical—the resting time. The term sabbatical comes from sabbath, or the day of rest in each week.

In the fifth chapter of Deuteronomy, the Lord told the Jews that they should work six days, but *"the seventh day is a sabbath . . ."* The meaning behind the sabbath is two-fold: The first is to set apart a day to honor the Lord; the second is to take a day a week to rest and recover. This practice was extended to include a sabbath year, called the year of remission, described in Deuteronomy 15:1-11.

This is not a book for an in-depth discussion of the sabbath day. Rather, I want to point out that God has provided a plan for His people to rest and recover *during* their working lives. As best I can determine, God has not prescribed a time when we should retire. We have arbitrarily decided that at age 62, 65, or some later period, our active working careers should stop. Nothing could be further from the truth, and we should begin to adjust to a saner and more reasonable philosophy.

Storing some funds during the most productive years of your life for the later years is both logical and biblical. As Proverbs 6:6 *says, "Go to the ant, O sluggard, observe her ways and be wise, which, having no chief, officer or ruler, prepares her food in the summer, and gathers her provision in the harvest."* Having some reserve allows you to take more frequent sabbaticals later in life or to volunteer your services to ministries without the necessity of being paid. But if you want to live the long, happy, healthy life that God has prescribed for you, don't retire!

Now, having stated my case against traditional retirement, I will rest it there and assume that you'll decide this issue before the Lord. From this point on, I'll conclude that the decision is yours.

The remainder of this book is dedicated to covering the decisions you'll be facing as the aging process continues. The only alternatives to the aging process are either the Lord's Second Coming, in which case nothing further is needed, or death, in which case retirement is not an issue.

*O*ne of the realities of retirement is that retirees become prospects for virtually every would-be financial advisor around—Christian and non-Christian alike. With the current lax rules on who can qualify as an investment advisor, it is prudent for retirees to learn enough so that they are not totally dependent on the counsel of others.

Retirement Realities

As I said in the last chapter, I will presume from this point that you have determined that at least some form of retirement, total or partial, is right for you, and therefore my function is to answer as many retirement questions as possible.

I would like to digress slightly and outline my personal philosophy on retirement. In doing so I hope to answer some of the expected questions that may arise from this book by those who earn their living selling retirement-oriented investments. I want to make it clear that I have thoroughly thought out my personal retirement goals. If the Lord allows me to retain my mental faculties and reasonably good health, I hope to continue working throughout my lifetime.

However, two considerations tend to shape my future economic decisions. First, there are no guarantees that I can continue to work at my current pace all of my life; so I may be forced to modify my traveling, teaching, and writing schedules. Second, I love to write more than any other thing I do and, therefore, I hope to be able to continue that work regardless of my age. Only the loss of my mental faculties would cause me to abandon that plan.

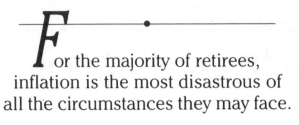

*F*or the majority of retirees,
inflation is the most disastrous of
all the circumstances they may face.

Because of what God has allowed me to do, I realize that I can develop a retirement plan that is significantly different than most. As long as people read books and a few are willing to buy those I write, my income can be generated through my labor rather than through investments. This is critically important because my need for retirement income through investments is less than for most others, and I don't have to do nearly as much long-term planning to cope with future inflation.

For the majority of retirees, inflation is the most disastrous of all the circumstances they may face. In a depressed economy, those living on fixed incomes may actually do better, since some prices tend to fall (assuming the retirees' source of income is dependable during that time). But inflation will eat the heart out of any retirement plan at a time when the retiree has little or no flexibility. I will address some methods to counter this problem in a later chapter.

Philosophically, I believe the first phase of any long-term financial goal should be to own your home *debt-free.* I am amazed how few people in our generation feel that owning their homes debt-free is important today. The practical truth is that having a debt-free home is better than earning the income to make the payments. No investment income is absolutely guaranteed, but mortgage payments are. The average mortgage payment in my area of the country is about $700 to $800 a month. For those who can itemize their deductions for tax purposes, this translates to approximately $500 to $600 in net costs. To earn that much through investments at an average rate of 10 percent would require at least $50,000 to $60,000 in investment capital and with no guarantees that the investments would be there in a bad economy.

My wife and I paid our home mortgage off in 1988, and I can say honestly that I have never regretted that decision; nor am I ever tempted to look at our home as "idle capital."

The second part of my financial philosophy is to put aside the equivalent of my previous house payment in a tax-sheltered plan each month. Because I am self-employed, I have the use of an SEP-IRA (Simplified Employee Pension–Individual Retirement Account) which allows me to put 15 percent of my net income (including the deductible contribution) into an SEP plan if I desire. I personally never put that much aside because my long-term goals don't require it. I believe the funds can be put to better use in God's work today.

I do not presume that my plan is the best for everyone. My goal is that, by age 65 (more or less), my long-term investments will provide approximately one-third of my annual income needs.

The third phase of my planning is to put approximately 10 percent of my net income into long-range investments—after taxes. It is my opinion that assets stored in qualified retirement accounts are extremely vulnerable to the whims and wishes of the politicians. As I have reviewed the needs of the Social Security system, I simply cannot see enough tax dollars available to keep the system solvent into the next century. I also believe the Social Security system is a "sacred cow" within political circles and will be maintained at all costs (except possibly for high-income retirees).

As I have reviewed the rising costs of Social Security and the declining sources of revenue, I've concluded that additional funding will be absolutely necessary. It's my *opinion* that private retirement accounts for middle and upper income workers are the most likely source of those funds. I realize that presently this isn't being debated in Washington, and most of the experts I talked with consider it highly unlikely that private retirement funds will be used to support the Social Security system. *I do not.*

In the quest for social program funds, nothing is beyond our politicians. They have broken existing contracts before, and I believe they will do so again. Therefore, my counsel to those saving for retirement in the twenty-first century is: Don't put your total retirement savings in a tax-sheltered plan—ever!

In order to be balanced about this particular aspect of long-term financial planning, I would ask anyone who does not share my particular perspective on this topic to reserve judgment until you finish this entire book, including the discussion on Social Security. Then put yourself in the place of politicians who have made impossible promises to future retirees, and decide what you would do if you had to make the decisions. If the government can remove the U.S. currency from the gold standard (which it did), confiscate private property for failure to pay taxes (which it does), and steal Social Security trust funds that are clearly earmarked for retirees (which it is doing), I doubt that anything is beyond possibility.

*T*he point that needs to be emphasized is that *nothing* is certain in the area of long-term financial planning.

In discussing the realities of retirement, it is important to note that many decisions other than investment decisions can dramatically affect your plans. For instance, I recently received a letter from a widow whose husband had retired from a major company two years earlier. She said that one of his options at retirement was either a single-life annuity with a higher monthly income, or a two-life annuity with a lower income. The two-life annuity would continue to pay her in the event of her husband's death. Since the two-life option had a lower monthly payout, her husband opted for the single-life plan. He died unexpectedly two years later, the annuity income ceased, and she was left with nothing but a small Social Security income to live on. As a result, she was forced to return to the job market in her mid-sixties in order to meet her minimum needs. As the old cliché says, he was penny wise and pound foolish.

In counseling many retirees I found that many seemingly non-investment decisions drastically altered their retirement plans.

Bill, an airline pilot, retired from a major airline company at age 60 with a pension income of nearly $40,000 a year in 1975. Forty thousand dollars a year was a fantastic retirement income in the mid-seventies. Because he had attained his retirement goal, Bill decided to cancel all of his personal life insurance, except a small burial policy. He had selected the two-life retirement benefit from the airlines so that his wife would receive his pension in the event something happened to him, so he felt his need for life insurance was negligible.

Unfortunately, in the late eighties, the airline went bankrupt and left much of the pension plan unfunded. Without a source of income from the parent company, the pension plan was forced to reduce the payout to its retirees. In Bill's case, this trimmed his retirement income by nearly one-half. The income was still adequate, provided Bill supplemented it by working part-time. Less than a year later Bill was diagnosed with terminal cancer and died within a few months. His wife was left with no insurance, a sizeable medical bill (since the company's medical plan was also eliminated), and not enough income to live on as Bill had planned. He had not anticipated the complete failure of the parent company and the retirement account as well.

The point that needs to be emphasized is that *nothing* is certain in the area of long-term financial planning. Bill assumed that since he was retired from a major corporation he was set for life. The decision to cancel his life insurance was made without considering the total consequences. Obviously it's not possible to foresee every possible scenario for the future, but the basic principles of long-term financial planning don't change all that much from one individual to another. Once you understand the basics, the decisions become easier. Just bear in mind the two rules of Murphy's Law: "Anything that can go wrong will go wrong" and "Murphy was an optimist."

In both of the previous examples, two basic principles were ignored: Wives outlive their husbands most of the time;

and, there should always be a fall-back plan if your total retirement income is invested in one area.

In the early 1980s a couple came to see me with a difficult situation. The husband, Ted, had retired from a computer company at age 62 and elected to take his retirement savings in a lump sum rather than a monthly annuity. With over $200,000 in hand, Ted set out to invest the money to supplement his Social Security income.

A Christian investment advisor in his church knew about his recent retirement and offered to help invest the money. With the best of intentions, and some very bad strategies, this man talked Ted into investing in the commodities market.[1] He convinced Ted that by investing in futures options he would be able to limit his liability while maximizing his return.

Ted was no dummy, but all of his business experience had been in selling computers and business equipment. Besides, the advisor was a Christian and had shown Ted some remarkable graphs demonstrating what (profit) he had made personally using the same strategy.

Let me pause for a moment to make a comment: I have seen many Christian financial advisors who, with the best of intentions, gave bad advice. Too often the investors placed unrealistic confidence in them because they were Christians. It's been my observation that Christians can give some pretty bad counsel. So be careful.

Ted began his retirement investing by risking initially only a small portion of his savings. In the first year, his average return was over 100 percent on the money invested. Gradually Ted increased his stake until he had nearly $150,000 at risk. What Ted didn't know was that his advisor had shifted his strategy from options, which limited Ted's exposure only to the money invested, to actual futures contracts, in which the profits were potentially enormous but so were the proportionate risks.

Obviously for a retiree like Ted, with virtually no experience, risking retirement money in options was illogical enough. But gambling on commodity futures would be illogical

1. For a discussion of commodity future options, see *Investing for the Future,* published by Victor Books.

for a 30-year-old with a $200,000 annual income. I've discussed the idea of commodities investing with Mark Ritchie, one of the major brokers on the Chicago Board of Trade. He estimates the odds of an amateur investor getting his money back (no profit) at 200-to-1. That doesn't make any sense—except for the broker.

You can probably guess the ultimate outcome in this case: A major shift in the commodities market caused the investments to plummet. The broker handling the contracts made a call to Ted's advisor for more collateral to cover the contracts (bought on margin), and Ted got a rude awakening.

Ted described a call he received one Friday morning from his investment advisor.

"Ted, we have a problem."

"What kind of problem?" Ted asked guardedly.

For several months Ted had known that something was wrong, although he didn't know exactly what. Several times in previous weeks the advisor had called to pressure Ted into increasing his investment—each time telling him about a great "opportunity" that couldn't wait. Each call resulted in Ted's risking several thousand dollars more. Initially Ted and his wife, June, had set a limit on what they would invest in any one area, but the profits from the option trading looked so good that Ted had continued to increase his percentage—without telling June.

At the insistence of his advisor, Ted had actually signed a limited power of attorney authorizing him to buy and sell in Ted's name. At the time, Ted had a check in his spirit about signing a power of attorney, but he had been assured that the document was necessary if they were to act swiftly on the opportunities available.

"It's for your protection," the advisor had counseled Ted as they ate lunch. "If something happened to me and all the contracts were in my name alone you'd have a terrible time getting your money out."

So, in spite of his better judgment, Ted signed the document, which was the equivalent of authorizing withdrawals from his savings account.

Ted decided not to mention it to June since she was already upset about the amount Ted was investing. Ted knew he was risking too much money in something she didn't understand. When he thought about it, which he tried not to do too often, Ted wasn't sure he understood it either.

Ted's attention returned to the call. "You'll need to put up some more money," he heard the advisor say.

"How much more money?" Ted asked with a tinge of alarm in his voice, "and why?"

"I'll need at least $50,000 today," the advisor stammered, trying his best to sound authoritative.

"Fifty thousand!" Ted shouted into the phone. "I don't have $50,000 now. All my money is tied up in these options. How could you need that much?"

"The broker who handles our trading has made more margin calls," his advisor replied defensively, trying to shift the blame to the broker.

"What exactly is a margin call?" Ted asked. "I thought you said I was only liable for the money I had at risk."

"Didn't you read the reports I sent you each month? They clearly showed that I shifted most of your account into commodities futures."

"I didn't understand one thing those papers said," Ted replied angrily. "If you'll remember, I asked you about them and you said not to worry—that you'd take care of all the details."

"I don't remember saying that," the advisor replied nervously. "But the bottom line is, you'll need to wire some money to the trading account immediately or the broker will sell your contracts and charge you for the losses."

The net result of Ted's trading was that he lost virtually all of the money he and his wife had worked so long to accumulate. Fortunately for Ted and June, the commodity brokerage firm decided not to sue for the contract deficiencies, which amounted to more than $30,000. The financial advisor eventually lost his securities license but, unfortunately, Ted was unable to recover any of his money since the man declared bankruptcy.

This situation was obviously traumatic for Ted and June. She felt that Ted had deceived her, or at least ignored her by not keeping her informed about what he was doing. In the period before I saw them, they also had accumulated several thousand dollars of credit card debt. Typical of many young (and older) couples in this situation, they supported themselves by using credit cards until that source ran out as well.

Fortunately for Ted and June, they had raised four godly children who stepped in to help. The children paid off the credit card debts, with the agreement that their parents would go for counseling. Over the next few months Ted began receiving his Social Security pension, and he was able to find a part-time job in a retail computer store. Their income stabilized at about $1,000 a month, or approximately one-third of Ted's pre-retirement income. They made the adjustment, but the lifestyle they had planned for all those years was modified drastically.

One of the realities of retirement is that retirees become prospects for virtually every would-be financial advisor around —Christian and non-Christian alike. With the current lax rules on who can qualify as an investment advisor, it is prudent for retirees to learn enough so that they are not totally dependent on the counsel of others. Even giving Ted's advisor the benefit of the doubt about his motives, his expertise and judgment were deficient.

Anyone can be duped by a slick salesperson. This is especially true when the salesperson presents himself or herself as a Christian and therefore is presumed to be ethical and honest. Unfortunately, as I said earlier, this is not always a logical presumption.

*N*othing in our economy
happens in a vacuum. Each time
a major player in the economy
fails, the ripple effect is
felt throughout the system.

CHAPTER THREE

Future Problems

It seems probable that we have seen the zenith of the American economy. I don't mean that all future generations will live in poverty; probably they won't. But future workers and retirees will face an increasingly difficult economy in which there will be fewer jobs at lower wages.

Many workers in the next century will discover that the social programs of the twentieth century came with a high price tag: future jobs. From the 1970s on, the politicians who engineered the entitlement programs lacked the courage to tell the American people the true cost of re-engineering our society. Instead they borrowed from future generations and stripped the economy of investment capital that would otherwise have gone into creating more jobs.

When the working people of the next century are asked to increase their "contributions" to support the baby boomers, the price simply will be too high. Consequently those people born after 1940 had better plan to expect less entitlements or the "me" generation of the sixties and seventies will probably seek out some creative ways to reduce their overhead.

Keep in mind that those who will be in control of our country in the next two decades have been raised on a steady diet of permissiveness, selfishness, and indulgence. If they won't tolerate the inconvenience of their own children, why would they tolerate the inconvenience of high costs for the elderly?

*B*y the turn of the century,
environmental restrictions will
force thousand of other companies
to close or relocate.

It seems obvious that the U.S. economy is shifting from an industrial base to a service industry base; and practically speaking, the service industries—fast foods, car repairs, computer services—don't pay the same wages as automobile manufacturing and steel production.

The United States may recapture isolated segments of lost markets, but our cost of labor, lower productivity, and lack of available capital make a large scale recovery of these basic industries almost impossible. The international investors get much better rates of return in developing countries, such as China, India, and Mexico, where the rules are more lax and the laws favor the company rather than the workers. Also the extremely high cost of litigation in America discourages new industries from starting here.

This can be evidenced by the demise of the private aircraft industry in the U.S. After leading the world in aviation technology and development for eighty years, the U.S. now has *no* private airplane manufacturers. Unlimited litigation, government regulation, and luxury taxes have eliminated more than 1,175,000 high-paying American jobs.

By the turn of the century, environmental restrictions will force thousand of other companies to close or relocate—many of them right across the border into Mexico, where the pollution will flow into the U.S. while the jobs flow into Mexico. Perhaps we'll see Americans sneaking across the border to find work in Mexico in the next century.

This is not to say that our country cannot reverse these trends. But it would seem unlikely, given the current mentality of our politicians and the reluctance of the social and environmental liberals to make the compromises necessary.

For those who will be facing retirement age in the twenty-first century, this is not just an academic discussion on the economy. The statistical facts are that more Americans are living longer and the employed ranks are growing slimmer.

As the graph below indicates, by the time today's children reach middle age, nearly 20 percent of the population will be over the age of 65; only 25 percent will be in the primary wage earners group (25-44).

The Narrowing Population Gap

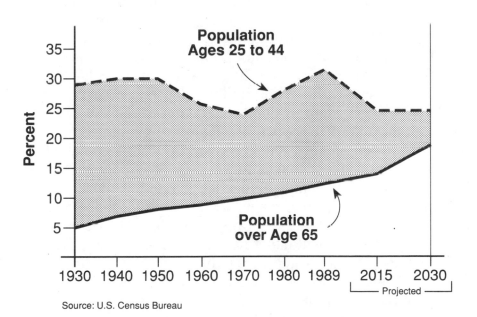

Source: U.S. Census Bureau

When the shift to a non-industrial base is factored into the next century, retirees will face some real challenges.

The Pension Benefit Guaranty Corporation (PBFC)

It is likely that many private retirement programs will fail during the decade of the nineties as the companies behind them either fail or withdraw from the U.S. work place. The PBGC is the federal agency that insures the private pension plans of approximately forty million Americans. The PBGC operates much like any other government insurance agency in that it has far fewer assets than liabilities—overwhelmingly so.

It should be noted that federal insurance plans—FDIC, FSLIC, FHA, VA, and the PBGC—were never meant to be total-cost insurers (meaning that they would guarantee all the liabilities of the funds they represent). It was assumed that the U.S. economy would be viable and growing and, at best, a few banks, savings and loans, or major companies might fail, necessitating these agencies to help only a fraction of the groups they insure. Instead we have seen a time-delayed "crash" of sorts in our economy. Big companies such as LTV, Eastern Airlines, and Pan American went bankrupt, leaving millions of dollars in unfunded pension liabilities. In addition, the collapse of the S&L industry burdened taxpayers with billions of dollars in unfunded depositor liabilities.

Nothing in our economy happens in a vacuum. Each time a major player in the economy fails, the ripple effect is felt throughout the system. With the federal government attempting to play the role of protector and trying to guarantee that no American loses any investment money, the unfunded liabilities continue to pile up. The real question is: What happens if several of these contingent liabilities fall due at the same time? It would seem that no one really wants to answer that question today. Considering the direction of our economy, it's a legitimate question that will either be addressed now, or later; and for retirees, later is not good enough.

I would like to focus attention on the PBGC briefly because it represents the typical problem retirees will be facing. The PBGC is little more than a government "shell game." On the surface the system looks sound enough. The agency was established as a fail-safe for pensioners whose retirement plans might go "belly up" because of company failures. It was recognized that many private pension plans were (and are) woefully underfunded. Quite often a parent company funds an employees' retirement account on a "pay-as-you-go" concept. As long as the company remains profitable, there is no problem. But once the company begins to lose money, the pension plan represents a significant cash drain. If the company files for bankruptcy protection, the drain is removed, but so is the employees' retirement income.

*T*oo often individuals tend to think the problems are so big that they can do nothing about them. I assure you that is not true. Just one person who has the correct facts and is willing to take on the establishment can make the difference.

In 1974 Congress created the PBGC to cover this contingency—well before the huge trade deficits of the late eighties and while the annual federal deficit was a mere $70 billion or so.

As of 1992 the total liabilities of the private pension system are about $900 billion; the assets total about $1.3 trillion. So it would seem the system is secure and adequately funded. But, if you will recall, the same assessment was made of the Savings and Loan industry in the early eighties. Unfortunately, whether it is banks or pension plans, the assets are often overvalued and, once the slide starts, the remaining assets lose much of their value quickly. As in the case of the S&Ls (an industry that boasted a total net worth of $600 billion as late as 1983), the failed "thrifts" actually had a combined deficit of some $500 billion once the collapse began.

In looking at the viability of any insurance program, it is important to look at the worst case scenario, not the best. Remember what Murphy's law says: If anything can go wrong, it will.

Granted, the overall pension system is solvent at this time; however, it is not possible to rob from the well-funded plans to give to the underfunded plans—according to existing law. (If that law were changed, the underfunded pension plans would quickly deplete the well-funded ones.) Consequently the PBGC has to be reviewed as if the underfunded plans will fail, leaving the agency to pick up the deficits. This is very revealing.

In 1990 the agency's single-employer pension plan had a total deficit of approximately $1.9 billion. By 1991 the *deficit* had increased to $2.5 billion—an increase of 32 percent.

But even this trend pales in comparison with the underfunded liabilities of major companies. In 1990 company pension plans were underfunded by approximately $30 billion. By the end of 1991 the deficit had risen to $40 billion. According to the Government Accounting Office, even this amount is significantly understated. The failed plans taken over by the PBGC in 1991 had their assets overstated by between 20 and 40 percent, while the liabilities were understated by some 37 percent. Logically, one can assume the same would be true of plans that have not yet failed.

Basically this means that the $70 billion line of credit issued to the PBGC by Congress could be depleted easily if the economy suffers any significant setbacks over the next ten years, as many economists expect it will.

From my review of the information released on the PBGC, the danger lies more in the next decade than in the present one. There are adequate reserves and loans that can be tapped to continue the system under normal conditions. It is the abnormal conditions that future retirees should be most concerned about. Those who are dependent on company-funded retirement accounts should get information on how their funds are invested and whether or not the company is allowed to "borrow" the funds for current expenses.

Because so many plans are underfunded, new laws now require that companies set aside reserves for future retirees.

However, this condition often is satisfied by purchasing an insurance company annuity to cover the future liabilities. In the wake of recent insurance company failures, it would be prudent to verify the rating of the insurance company issuing the annuity.

Too often individuals tend to think the problems are so big that they can do nothing about them. I assure you that is not true. Just one person who has the correct facts and is willing to take on the establishment can make the difference. If you find your company plan is underfunded, you need to start a campaign to get it corrected—now. That means writing the company officials, calling and writing your elected representatives, and educating others who will be affected.

The most important action any of us can take is to pray. The Lord tells us in Matthew 6:31: *"Do not be anxious then, saying, 'What shall we eat?' or 'What shall we drink?' or 'With what shall we clothe ourselves?'"* And then in verse 34: *"Therefore do not be anxious for tomorrow; for tomorrow will take care for itself. Each day has enough trouble of its own."*

I interpret these passages to say that we are to trust God in the midst of chaos. But does this mean that we are to do nothing to help avoid a calamity? In Proverbs 27:12 God's Word also says: *"A prudent man sees evil and hides himself, the naive proceed and pay the penalty."* I believe this means that we should try to avoid being part of the problem—if at all possible.

The Problem of Health Insurance

The ever increasing cost of medical care has to be one of the primary concerns of any older person, especially a retiree. Since the implementation of Medicare in 1965, most older Americans have had their basic medical expenses insured through that system. But there are approximately six million people over the age of 65 who are not covered by any type of health plan. Some can qualify for Medicaid, the state-run medical supplement plan, but others cannot meet the qualifications because of income or other factors. Medicaid and Medicare provisions are discussed in Chapter 7 so I won't spend time discussing them here.

One observation that must be made, however, is that both Medicare and Medicaid *will* be reformed in some fashion over the next few years. Any discussion of these programs will have to be updated periodically as the laws are revised.

The cost of maintaining these programs in their current form will be impossible as more baby boomers approach retirement age and the economy adjusts downward to a service-oriented system. Again I repeat: I don't expect those who are already in the system to be dropped (except perhaps the higher-income retirees).

The political climate in our country makes changes to existing retirees' benefits almost sacred. Certainly our politicians are aware of the voting power of older Americans, and the fact that they do vote in greater numbers than any other age group makes them an imposing political group. Perhaps the one change that will be adopted is to remove the automatic cost of living adjustments that force the annual deficits ever higher.

I have heard it said that once the government decides to manage the health care system it will conform to government norms: Your local doctor's office will have the courtesy of the IRS, the efficiency of the Post Office, and the cost of the Pentagon.

The fact is, a health care system which cannot be supported financially but also cannot be changed spells disaster. To adequately fund the Medicare portion of Social Security will require massive influxes of new tax dollars. If the current trend in costs is not controlled, the health insurance funds will run out near the end of this decade. The following is a quote from the 1991 "Annual Report of the Medicare Board of Trustees."

There are currently over four covered workers support-
ing each HI [Hospital Insurance] enrollee. This ratio will begin
to decline rapidly early in the next century. By the middle of
that century, there will be only about two covered workers sup-
porting each enrollee. Not only are the anticipated reserves
and financing of the HI program inadequate to offset this demographic change, but under all but the most optimistic assumptions, the trust fund is projected to become exhausted
even before the major demographic shift begins to occur. Ex-
haustion of the fund is projected to occur shortly after the turn
of the century under the intermediate assumptions, and could
occur as early as 2001 if the pessimistic assumptions are
realized.

This virtually assures those not already in the system that
fundamental changes will be made before they qualify for
benefits. It is anybody's guess what changes will be made, but
almost certainly some form of national health care will be
implemented.

The obvious question has to be: If we already can't afford
the smaller system (Medicare/Medicaid), how will we be able
to afford a larger scale system? The answer is: We won't be able
to, but we'll do it anyway. This added cost may well drive the
last nails into our economic coffin. I have heard it said that
once the government decides to manage the health care system
it will conform to government norms: Your local doctor's office
will have the courtesy of the IRS, the efficiency of the Post Office, and the cost of the Pentagon.

ALTERNATIVE CHOICES

Until the actual changes are made to our health care system, it is impossible for me to comment on them. But as of this
time there are some viable alternatives for those who are not
covered under Medicare and expect to retire in the next few
years. If you are covered and have questions about supplemental insurance coverage, that will be discussed in Chapter 8.

Major Medical Plans

Retirees with good health can usually qualify for individual health insurance. Normally the cost of a full coverage policy is prohibitively expensive for most retirees. However, policies that pay primarily for major expenses, called major medical plans, are generally less expensive. That does not mean they are cheap; no health plan is cheap anymore. But the savings can range from 50 to 60 percent when compared with a full coverage plan.

The purpose of a major medical plan is to protect your assets from a catastrophic expense that would either deplete your savings or put you in debt for years. A single major health expense, such as a heart by-pass operation or cancer surgery, can easily do this.

Selecting both the policy and the issuing company is very important. Buying the cheapest plan may be "penny wise and pound foolish." The first priority is to have a company that will pay off when you have the need. Selecting a policy based only on the initial cost can lead to a bad experience when that need arises. Some companies thrive on litigation and find it less costly to retain attorneys than to pay legitimate claims.

*S*ome good advice for any potential retiree is, buy quality in health care providers, not initial costs; and always check the rating of your provider with the recognized rating services.

One couple I met in Atlanta discovered the hard way that there's a lot more to medical insurance than just the monthly premiums.

Roger and Nancy had lived most of their thirty years of marriage with virtually no medical expenses. When the 1990 recession began, Roger was a professional architect for a large commercial construction firm. His company was hit very hard by the downturn and, eventually, Roger realized that his position would be eliminated. Rather than wait for the inevitable, Roger accepted a voluntary early retirement from the company. He felt that he could easily earn a living until he was 62, at which time he would qualify for both Social Security and a pension from his company's 401(k) retirement plan. He had the option of continuing the company's health care insurance under the COBRA Act for eighteen months. But after reviewing the costs he and Nancy determined it would be better to purchase their own policy at a much lower premium.

They contacted an insurance agent within their church and viewed an array of policies. Each policy offered different benefits, and most were so confusing that Roger and Nancy scarcely understood the exclusions, much less the actual coverage. Eventually they decided just to tell the agent what coverage they wanted and what they could afford. Essentially they wanted a major medical plan that would protect them against potentially catastrophic medical bills.

The agent suggested a $1,000 deductible plan that would pay 80 percent of any hospital-related bills. He narrowed the choices down to two companies with about the same benefits, but the premiums of one company were less than half of the other.

When Roger questioned the difference in costs, the agent replied, "The smaller company is trying to buy into the market, so they're giving some very low rates up front."

"But won't they raise the rates later?" Nancy asked.

"Probably so," the agent agreed, "but we can lock in the lower rates for three years, and even then they won't be able to increase them much," he added. "If they do we'll just shop around for another company."

Obviously Roger should have questioned the wisdom of that advice. The logical questions he should have asked were: "What would the policy rates be if either of us were no longer insurable?" and "How long has this company been in the health insurance business?" But since Roger had always been a part of a group insurance plan, he didn't really know the right questions to ask; so he chose the cheaper policy.

A few months after Roger left his job, Nancy began to experience some dizzy spells. After repeated visits to her own doctor and several specialists, she was diagnosed with a rare blood disorder that required extensive hospitalization.

The medical bills for three months of care came to nearly $230,000. Their deductible and co-insurance costs were nearly $45,000. The sum was staggering but, since they had saved diligently most of their lives, it was at least manageable. Roger had been doing some consulting work, and he felt they could pay their portion off in less than two years.

But when the hospital and doctors began sending notices that the insurance company had not paid on any claims, Roger contacted the company in California. He had a sinking feeling when the operator responded, "The number you are calling is no longer in service."

Frantically Roger contacted his agent, who then contacted the state of California's insurance commissioner's office.

"The company has declared bankruptcy," the polite woman in the commissioner's office told him. "They have nearly $3 million in unpaid claims. You can file with the bankruptcy court but our investigation shows that the company has virtually no assets."

The trustee's report later verified that the company had no viable assets to cover its liabilities. The company had been in financial trouble even when Roger was evaluating their policy. Although the information was not disseminated widely, several insurance company rating services had listed them on their "problem" circular. Had the agent taken the time to verify some of these sources, he could have advised Roger and Nancy better. But he didn't.

Roger quickly learned that his obligations to the doctors and hospital were not contingent on his contract with the now-defunct insurance company. He still owed the health providers, irrespective of whether or not the insurance company paid him.

The state of California had a pooled fund to help cover the deficits of failed insurance companies, but the claims from within the state took priority. Once all the other debts were settled, Roger still owed a great deal more than he could ever hope to pay on a retirement income. Also, by that time Nancy was no longer insurable, and the bills continued to pile up.

Fortunately for Roger he was still relatively young and had a marketable skill that allowed him to reenter the work force. He was able to secure a job with a commercial construction company that provided group health insurance, so Nancy was covered once again. His retirement plans were put on hold for several years, but at least he was able to salvage some of his life savings.

Some retirees are not so fortunate. Some good advice for any potential retiree is, buy quality in health care providers, not initial costs; and always check the rating of your provider with the recognized rating services. Most of them can be found in your local library (see the Appendix for a listing of these services).

A Biblical Alternative

Outside of Medicare, Medicaid, or national health insurance, there are very few alternatives available for those approaching retirement age. However, for some, the alternative may be a biblically based plan, such as the Brotherhood Newsletter or the Good Samaritan Fund. When I first heard about these plans, I was skeptical. I have seen just about every kind of scam imaginable being promoted in the name of Christ—everything from engines that supposedly run on water to miracle healing gloves. So naturally I was more than a little cautious.

As I began to investigate the idea of Christians pooling their funds to provide health care for one another, I was impressed by the soundness of the concept.

In 2 Corinthians 8:14-15 the apostle Paul said: *"At the present time your abundance being a supply for their want, that their abundance also may become a supply for your want, that there may be equality; as it is written, 'He who gathered much did not have too much, and he who gathered little had no lack.'"* This is the principle upon which all the insurance companies in the world are built. It basically means that in any large group there will always be more healthy people than sick and more people living than dying. In insurance terms the principle is called actuarial probabilities: It is probable that more will be paid into a group plan than will be consumed.

The founder of the Brotherhood Newsletter, Bruce Hawthorn, took the passage in Corinthians literally and established a plan whereby Christians would band together and pay each others' medical bills. The principle is deceptively simple: If the group is large enough and most of the people in the group are healthy (on the average), they should be able to pay the costs of caring for those who are ill.

Each month the Brotherhood receives the medical bills from its members, spreads them across the entire group, and each member mails a small amount to the person assigned to him or her.

For example, let's assume that I join the group and agree to voluntarily send a gift of up to $50 a month to any other member who has a medical bill. If one member has a bill of $500, it would take ten members, each mailing $50, to cover that expense. Later, if I incur an expense of $500, ten members would do the same for me. As long as most of the members are well, the system works.

The same principle applies to all insurance companies. The only difference is that the insurance companies keep the surplus (their profit) and absorb the losses, if there are any. In truth, most insurance companies rarely take losses on their health coverage premiums since any losses in one year are passed along in the way of higher premiums the next year. The losses incurred by most insurance companies are in their investment portfolios, not in their benefits plans.

As of the date of this writing, the Brotherhood Newsletter has approximately 12,000 members, making it the largest self-help plan in the world (that I know of). The system seems to be functioning well and all the bills to date have been paid.

There is no guarantee that this plan, or a similarly structured plan called the Good Samaritan Plan, will withstand the assaults by insurance companies or by state insurance commissioners. The insurance business is highly competitive, and their legal departments are well funded. Most do not welcome any new competitors, especially Christian ones. Both the Brotherhood and Good Samaritan plans are regularly involved in defensive actions in various states.

There are restrictions in joining both the Brotherhood and the Good Samaritan Plan that limit their applicability to many people. To join, members must be Christians, nondrinkers, nonsmokers, and attend church regularly. Additionally, some pre-existing conditions are excluded from coverage, just as there would be in a qualifying health plan. But for those who can qualify and have no other affordable coverage, the plans represent an idea whose time has come. In an era when individual health policies can cost hundreds of dollars a month, these plans represent a viable alternative (see the Appendix for details on how to contact the Brotherhood Newsletter or Good Samaritan Plan).

NOTE: The author has no affiliation with either the Brotherhood Newsletter or the Good Samaritan Plan. Nor does the author give any endorsement of these plans in the future. All the information presented here was provided by the Brotherhood Newsletter and the Good Samaritan Plan without certified financial reports. The reader should rely on independent counsel before deciding on any health insurance provider.

A prudent man looks ahead and sees the problem and tries to avoid it, while the naive proceed without caution and pay the penalty (a paraphrase of Proverbs 27:12).

CHAPTER FOUR

When to Start a Retirement Plan

As I mentioned previously, one theory of retirement planning is to start at the earliest possible age. The logic behind this thinking is twofold: First, the younger you are, the more time you have to save for retirement; and, obviously, the more time you have, the more your savings will compound. The second reason for starting early is that it develops a habit of regular savings—a habit most Americans sorely need.

I can't fault the logic of starting a savings plan early. It's both biblical and practical. In Proverbs 21:20 we are told, *"There is precious oil and treasure in the dwelling of the wise, but a foolish man swallows it up."* Simply put, this means that wise people save a part of their earnings.

When it comes to *retirement* savings, though, I see two difficulties with the philosophy of starting at a young age.

First, it's very difficult to determine what will be a good investment in thirty years or so. Of course you can invest in areas that will allow you to shift your strategy as the economy changes. But for most average investors, that rarely works out.

Either they shift too soon or too late. Usually by the time word of a problem in the market reaches the general public, the parade has already passed (so to speak).

The second problem is what I call the "communications" factor in marriage. Usually husbands and wives have totally different perspectives on the use of surplus funds in their early years—at least where retirement is concerned. The husband may see retirement planning as a noble and achievable goal, but his wife is generally more interested in houses and furniture during these years. Until some of the more basic goals are achieved, any attempt to start a retirement plan is usually met with something less than enthusiasm by the wife. In no way am I trying to imply that saving money isn't important during these early years. It is. But other than a savings account for basic emergencies (four to six months of income), I believe the primary savings should be in debt reduction—not retirement planning.

STRATEGIES

In a previous book I wrote, *Investing for the Future,* I discussed the strategies of investing according to the seasons of life, so I won't elaborate here; but I feel the necessity to at least explain the concept for those who have not read that book. If you look at age in terms of the seasons of life, it will help develop some realistic goals for what you want to accomplish financially prior to retirement.

*T*here is no trick to good financial planning. It is simply a matter of establishing priorities and sticking to them.

This discussion would be much simpler if I were addressing either a group of college seniors or a group of retirees (individuals who are all about the same age and on somewhat equal footing financially). Unfortunately, that is not the case. I know some readers will be in the 20 to 40 year old range, and others will be the 60 to 80 age group. Still others probably are somewhere between those two. Some of you have stored sizeable amounts of money already, while others are approaching their retirement years with little or nothing in savings.

According to the Social Security Administration, less than 2 percent of all 60 year old adults in America are financially secure. They can support themselves (including Social Security) with an income the equivalent of the average American family ($28,000/year). According to the same source, approximately 60 percent of all 65 year old retirees still have mortgages on their homes. The average length of their mortgages is eighteen years. That's pretty optimistic for a 65 year old. It's also pretty alarming for their economic future.

THE SPRING SEASON—AGES 20 to 40

During these early years most young families are concerned with building careers and families. Their financial goals should revolve around having adequate life insurance, buying debt-free automobiles, starting college funds for their children, and paying off their home mortgages. Assuming that each of these areas are kept in balance, any couple can be debt-free (mortgage included) by age 40, provided they make this a high priority.

SUMMER SEASON—AGES 40 TO 60

Once the car(s) and home(s) are debt-free, there should be sufficient funds available to pay for most of their children's college expenses from freed monthly income—provided the money is not diverted into indulgences like bigger homes, boats, vacations, and such.

One point should be made: There is no trick to good financial planning. It is simply a matter of establishing priorities and sticking to them. A short-term indulgence, such as a new car every four or five years, translates into tens of thousands of dollars consumed that cannot be recovered.

Good financial planning does not exclude all new cars or better homes forever. It simply means prioritizing goals. As Proverbs 28:22 says: *"A man with an evil eye hastens after wealth, and does not know that want will come upon him."* Unfortunately this concept is not taught much anymore, particularly in a society that depends on debt-ridden consumers.

*D*ebt retirement is one of the few absolutely guaranteed investments you can make in this or any other economy.

Some time ago I had the privilege of interviewing Sir John Templeton, founder of the multi-billion dollar Templeton Mutual Funds company. I asked Mr. Templeton, "To what do you attribute your great success?"

His reply was, "The Lord and disciplined saving." He went on to describe how he and his wife had saved 50 percent of their meager earnings early in their married life. They once furnished an apartment for $25 by buying at auctions and second-hand stores. He limited his lifestyle early in his life in order to accomplish greater goals later, which he did.

Mr. Templeton also shared that he avoided the use of debt to the highest degree possible throughout his career. The only loan he ever had was a $10,000 note to help capitalize his investment company. He drove used cars, lived in rented apartments, and rarely ate out until his income was well established.

Not everyone has been gifted with the abilities of John Templeton, but anyone can apply basic financial principles to his finances—especially that of saving to make purchases, rather than continually going into debt.

The 40 to 60 season should be the time for paying off all outstanding debts, including your home. I realize this counsel will often run contrary to the advice of other financial counselors; but bear in mind that those counselors don't have to make your mortgage payments if you hit a financial setback. Debt retirement is one of the few absolutely guaranteed investments you can make in this or any other economy. During a bad economy you may not be able to find your investment advisors, or even the companies you invest with, but the certainty is, you won't have any difficulty locating your mortgage company.

> *T*oo often in our generation people are looking to the government to meet their needs in the "fall" years of their lives.

One of the greatest temptations most Americans face at this stage of life is lifestyle adjustment. Usually this is the time when incomes have peaked and expenses have declined. The children are gone, or leaving, and most of the college expenses are behind. This is the single greatest opportunity to develop the surpluses to invest (or give), but unfortunately most Americans use the potential surpluses to buy motor homes, take more expensive vacations, buy bigger houses, and generally indulge themselves. The result is clearly seen in the next season of life.

THE FALL SEASON: AGE 60 PLUS

By age 60 most Americans could be debt-free and have some significant surpluses available for retirement. It is a statistical fact however that relatively few do. Too often in our generation people are looking to the government to meet their needs in the "fall" years of their lives. When the government proves unable to do so (as they ultimately must), many will be facing some harsh realities, not the least of which will be returning to the job market with decreased capacities and outdated skills.

If you're in this situation beyond the age of 60, there is not much I can say or do in this book that will help you. There is no easy fix for the lack of financial discipline discussed so thoroughly in God's Word. Perhaps Proverbs 13:18 best describes this principle, *"Poverty and shame will come to him who neglects discipline.*

Obviously one word of encouragement I can offer is that God forgives our transgressions, including our lack of discipline. He also promises not to forsake us, even in the financial area. But nowhere in God's Word does He promise to restore the wasted years or the squandered resources. All too often a reduced living standard is the consequence of earlier wrong decisions.

The 60-plus season is the time to begin shifting from the accumulation to the conservation mode. This generally holds true for the majority of people, although there will always be some exceptions, such as Harland Sanders of Kentucky Fried Chicken. For most people over the age of 60, the funds earned at an earlier age cannot be replaced if lost, so *caution* is the key term.

I wish that I could require every 40 year old in America to counsel with a few retirees who have done the wrong things financially and are suffering with their consequences. Perhaps it would shock some of the younger group into using more common sense. Suffice it to say that a prudent man looks ahead and sees the problem and tries to avoid it, while the naive proceed without caution and pay the penalty (a paraphrase of Proverbs 27:12).

Those who are 60 and older need to adopt a balanced, conservative investment policy. That does not mean no risks; but it certainly does mean no foolish risks.

A retiree, whom I'll call Jack, had been a successful salesman most of his working career. He took an early retirement at age 59 with the idea that he would play golf, start a garden, and putter around in the yard when he needed to fill in some time.

What Jack failed to take into account was that rarely does a 59 year old man just shut down his work motivation, as he was attempting to do. Within six months he was bored out of his mind and looking for something to do.

Unfortunately Jack had always made most of the financial decisions in his family, with little or no input from his wife. When he was working he was able to cover his remarkably consistent string of mistakes by generating more income. Most of his losses went undetected by his wife, although she had a strong suspicion that several investments had gone sour—especially when Jack worked harder for a while.

Jack met an energetic young businessman in the swap shop newspaper business during a Saturday golf game. He shared with Jack his great idea for developing a new business: a computerized swap shop.

The basic concept was very good. He would combine all the neighborhood swap shop newsletters and merge them into one computerized system, thereby matching buyers and sellers from all areas of the city. All he lacked, he said, was adequate capital to develop the computer software.

Jack recognized the potential in the younger man's idea and provided the initial $25,000 in funding. Had his investment been limited to no more than the original $25,000, Jack could have sustained that loss without doing irreparable harm to his retirement income. But, as you might guess, the investment grew as the idea developed, until Jack had nearly $300,000 invested—virtually all the capital he had saved.

The need for additional funding didn't arise the first week. It developed as the idea developed, and Jack supplied progressively more money to protect the money he had already loaned.

In this case, the idea really was good and the potential business quite viable. But the amount of capital it would have taken to develop the software and buy the necessary equipment was at least twice what Jack was able to provide. When his money ran out Jack was left with little more than a distant hope that he would ever get even a portion of his investment back. The one thing he was left with was a very hurt and angry wife who felt she had been betrayed by her husband of thirty years.

Jack went back to work, which was probably the best thing for him at that time anyway. His guilt over having lost the money and having alienated his wife helped him get his priorities in order. I met them because Jack had committed to live on a budget for the first time in his life, and he committed also to include his wife in every decision he made from that point on.

Fortunately, in Jack's case, he later recovered nearly $100,000 of his money when a large company purchased the idea that had been developed. He and his wife decided to reinvest $25,000 in the company that took over the project. During the next several years that investment also grew to nearly $100,000.

WHEN TO INVEST?

I would like to stop here and once again address the issue of when to start a retirement program. As you might guess, it is very difficult to start an effective retirement plan after the age of 60. Colonel Sanders was 66 when he started his first Kentucky Fried Chicken franchise (now known as KFC), and he has become a positive role model for older Americans. It would be naive to think that every retiree might follow in his tracks. Most people simply lack the time and income to develop a significant surplus beyond the age of 60—but some could.

I want to emphasize that the one *sure* investment that anyone can make is to give to the Lord's work. God said that an investment in His kingdom will return one hundred-fold. That's a 10,000 percent return!

I previously stated that my advice to young investors (ages 20 to 40) is to concentrate on debt reduction. So the majority of actual pre-retirement planning will be relegated to the 40 to 60 age range for two reasons: One, that's the age when the income is greatest and some risks can be assumed; and two, that's the biggest group of Americans alive today. I seriously doubt that it is possible to look ahead twenty years and develop any realistic financial plans, given our current economic situation. But as noted previously, if you wait too long time will eliminate your options, so you need to start now, trust the Lord for wisdom, and stay flexible.

If our economy fails during the next ten years, your best efforts probably will be futile; but those options are in the Lord's hands, not ours. We are directed to do the best we can with what we have, including our limited knowledge of the future.

I want to emphasize that the one *sure* investment that anyone can make is to give to the Lord's work. God said that an investment in His kingdom will return one hundredfold. That's a 10,000 percent return! My suggestion is to ask the Lord to reinvest the dividends for you and allow you to collect them in heaven. Then you will have an eternity to enjoy the fruits of your labors.

*S*ome time ago I read a study done by Harvard University on 200 of their 65 year old male graduates, 100 of whom retired and another 100 who did not. At age 75, seven out of eight of the retirees had died, while seven out of eight of the non-retirees were still alive and well.

CHAPTER FIVE

Who Should Retire?

The option of early retirement is being offered to more and more older employees as companies attempt to pare down their work forces. Many companies offer lucrative bonuses to entice higher-paid employees to retire early because it reduces their fixed overhead—a good option for many bloated companies. But is early retirement a good deal for the retirees? The answer is: It depends.

TEMPERAMENT

Temperament is a vital factor to consider when you're facing a retirement decision. Some people seem able to adjust to retirement better than others. Usually these are the Type B personalities. Type B people are those who generally are more laid back or easygoing individuals. The Type A personalities (like me) are more aggressive, and they are more project oriented. Adjusting to retirement is often traumatic for the Type A.

If you're not familiar with the terms "Type A" and "Type B" personalities, let me explain. A Type B personality is often characterized as a "people person," and a Type A as a "task person." A Type B personality seems able to adapt to a slower pace more readily than a Type A because the latter needs new challenges regularly (I should know).

It is much better to determine which description best fits you before you retire, rather than later.

*I*f the wife of a husband about to retire dreads the day when he will sit around the house telling her how to clean more efficiently, he's probably a Type A.

Allow me to make a few non-scientific comparisons about these two personalities. But first I'll preface my statements with one observation: No one is an either/or personality; we are all a mixture of several types. But for simplicity's sake, I will limit my discussion to the primary characteristics.

I also realize that any thorough analysis would cover more than just two types of personalities. In our counseling ministry we use a simple test that measures four basic personality types. Even so, it is my opinion that most of us can be classified as either basically a Type A or Type B. For example, my doctor tends to qualify everything he tells me with the statement, "I know that as a Type A you always question everything, so here's some research data on . . . (whatever the topic is).

TYPE A PERSONALITY

Those who question if they are Type A personalities have only to ask their spouses to find out. If the wife of a husband about to retire dreads the day when he will sit around the house telling her how to clean more efficiently, he's probably a Type A.

*A*ll of the traits that make Type A personalities good leaders in the work place tend to work against them in retirement.

Retirement can be a death sentence for the Type A personalities. As I said, they are task-oriented, performance-driven people and without challenges they tend to depress easily. Even worse, without goals they tend to become more introverted and easily irritated, even with those they love the most.

Following are a few of the more common Type A personality characteristics.

- They seek immediate challenges and results.
- They make decisions easily, even if they're the wrong ones.
- They hate the status quo and require a variety of different tasks regularly.
- They tend to assume authority easily.
- They like to manage a variety of tasks simultaneously.
- They thrive on problems.

All of the traits that make Type A personalities good leaders in the work place tend to work against them in retirement. Unless they have very specific (and realistic) goals at retirement that include staying active in some type of work, the result is often too much internal stress and usually health problems. Rarely will a Type A person marry another Type A. If they do, the relationship is often described as "hammers and knives at short distances."

My wife is a Type B, and the differences in our personalities never cease to amaze me. Usually I find myself envious of her ability to relax and adjust quickly. Not me. It takes me three or four days after starting a vacation before I can relax, and when I drive, I find myself setting personal goals to see how quickly I can get from one place to another. Stopping just to "look" is anathema to a Type A. We must be taught to relax.

When I walk it is always for exercise, and I compete against the clock. My wife loves to stroll, while I charge ahead. Recently we walked my daily exercise route together. Along the way she pointed out a variety of flowers and even a lake that I had never noticed, even though I walk the same route every day. When I walk I'm not out to look at the scenery; I'm there to *walk!* The next day, when I walked alone, I found it enlightening to notice that there were trees, bushes, and even flowers along my path.

It has been suggested that Type A personalities are actually insecure people who are constantly striving to prove they're worthy. As a Type A myself, I suspect this is true to varying degrees for most of us. By personality a Type A is both competitive and rarely content unless involved in a project. Obviously this characteristic should be controlled under the influence of the Holy Spirit, but the underlying personality is always there.

It is important for those with Type A personalities to recognize why God has designed them this way. They are the "movers and shakers"—the "planners and dreamers," if you will. But, as I said, retirement for a Type A is traumatic, and sometimes fatal. Don't make your retirement plans based on what someone else has done. The person you're attempting to emulate may have the personality to adjust to a life of trivia and little real productivity. You may not!

TYPE A PERSONALITY TEST

The following is a condensed self-test for a Type A personality. If many or most of these definitions fit your personality (or your spouse's) you should NEVER plan to withdraw totally from the work place.

1. Tend to make quick decisions, and influence others to follow.
   Yes _____   No _____

2. Tend to interrupt others who drag out an explanation.
   Yes _____   No _____

3. More project-oriented then people-oriented.
   Yes _____   No _____

4. Tend to work on several projects at one time (often over-committing myself).
   Yes _____   No _____

5. Would rather be a "quarterback" than a lineman.
   Yes _____   No _____

6. Tend to feel depressed if not successful regularly.
   Yes _____   No _____

7. Tend to be the problem solver of the family or business.
   Yes _____   No _____

8. Will run a stop light at 2:00 A.M. rather than wait for the light to change.
   Yes _____   No _____

9. Will drive out of the way to avoid stop lights, even if the route is longer.
   Yes _____   No _____

10. Will rarely stop on family trips (even to use the rest room).
    Yes _____   No _____

11. An early riser, and a late nighter.
    Yes _____   No _____

12. Will rarely read an instruction manual before attempting a project.
    Yes _____   No _____

13. Have a poor sense of direction, but hesitate to ask others for directions (a sign of weakness).
    Yes _____   No _____

14. Tend to have mood swings apparent to others, but seldom recognize them.
    Yes _____   No _____

15. Very sensitive, but with a gruff exterior.

Yes _____   No _____

If you answered ten or more of these questions *yes,* you are most certainly a Type A. You need to stay active at any age. Retirement can be a change of careers, perhaps even a phase-down time, but traditional retirement will traumatize you.

Some time ago I read a study done by Harvard University on 200 of their 65 year old male graduates, 100 of whom retired and another 100 who did not. At age 75, seven out of eight of the retirees had died, while seven out of eight of the non-retirees were still alive and well. After eliminating outside factors, such as illness, the conclusion the researchers reached was: Most died of terminal boredom.

Type B Personality

I have often admired Type B personalities because they seem to be able to stop and smell the flowers (so to speak) more than Type A personalities do. But the very characteristics that help them to adjust to daily routines and control their stress often work against them in a crisis situation.

*T*he ability to accept circumstances that cannot be changed is an admirable trait. The acceptance of circumstances that could be changed through some personal effort is slothfulness.

Let me share an example: Some time ago I spoke at a large church where the pastor was clearly a Type A. That evening we had dinner with one of the church deacons, who was clearly a Type B. Both the pastor and the deacon had gone through heart-bypass surgery in the previous five years. The Type A pastor was obviously watching his diet carefully and described in detail his regular exercise routine. Not only was he counting calories but could estimate the amount of fat in each item on the menu.

The Type B deacon, however, was oblivious to anything but the most basic understanding of the fat content of the food he ordered, and even the warnings of his pastor did not dissuade him from eating what he wanted.

When the pastor counseled him on the need to watch his diet and control his cholesterol intake he retorted, "Why? If I have another problem I can always have another bypass."

This fundamental attitude difference explains a lot about the adaptability of a Type A and a Type B. The Type A is a competitor, highly motivated by a challenge, including heart disease. The Type B will adjust to most situations and treat many difficulties as inevitable.

Unfortunately, in the case of retirement this often translates into doing little or no preparation and then living at or near the poverty level. The ability to accept circumstances that cannot be changed is an admirable trait. The acceptance of circumstances that could be changed through some personal effort is slothfulness.

Following is a brief self-evaluation for a Type B personality.

1. Tend to put off major tasks rather than spend the time planning.
    Yes _____   No _____

2. Motivated to a high degree by the appreciation of others.
    Yes _____   No _____

3. Generally a good listener.
    Yes _____   No _____

4. Tend to be too compliant with people who abuse me.
    Yes _____   No _____

5. Find contentment in minor tasks such as yard work, home maintenance, or similar tasks.
    Yes _____   No _____

6. Will work at the pace of others around me rather than risk offending them.

    Yes _____   No _____

7. Adapt well to modern retirement, but often lose contact with lifetime goals.

    Yes _____   No _____

8. Usually accept the idea that most things really can't be changed by me.

    Yes _____   No _____

9. Tend to be more complacent financially; will have unpaid debts at retirement.

    Yes _____   No _____

10. More family oriented.

    Yes _____   No _____

If you answered at least seven out of the ten questions affirmatively, you qualify as a Type B. The primary negative of this personality is the tendency to procrastinate and lean on the counsel of others too much.

Again, I look at the difference in my wife and me in this regard. She accepts implicitly the counsel of her doctor because he represents an authority figure. On the other hand, I require statistical proof of any diagnosis and will evaluate other resources and studies on my own before agreeing to any procedure. The negative aspect of this is that I'll delay going to my doctor until all else fails, while my wife will seek counsel much sooner.

For each personality type, any retirement planning must entail some realistic self-evaluation. The Type A must realize that any period of time without goals and achievements will usually lead to frustration and discontentment. For these people, leaving one phase of life can only be successful if specific goals are established for the next. To think that a task-motivated individual will be satisfied with working in the yard and playing golf twice a week is foolish. Perhaps volunteering with a non-profit organization is a good alternative, provided there is at least some degree of control over the tasks.

I recall a friend who found out about retirement the hard way after retiring from the military as a field grade officer. Initially he and his wife bought a motor home to travel the country "smelling all the roses" he had missed in twenty-three years of traveling throughout the world in the armed services. According to his wife, their leisurely travel lasted about four months, and then he became more and more restless.

His next project was to buy a home in Florida and take up golf seriously. So for about six months he attacked the game, practicing his putting and drives for up to four hours a day. Then when he hit the links with some of the other retirees, he discovered it bored him terribly.

Next he sold the home in Florida and moved to North Carolina, where he took up painting, and for the next few months he attended art classes and studied the masters. But after ten or twelve paintings (pretty good ones), he decided that too was boring and their home in the Carolinas was too much work. So he sold that home and headed for Bible college.

I could go on with his story for at least five more ventures. Finally he decided that he needed to go back to work, so he volunteered as the facility manager at a church in Georgia. This lasted for about a year and a half—until his ideas conflicted with the senior pastor's. Then he found himself being ignored more and more frequently.

This led to a feeling of low self-esteem and bouts of depression. He began to doubt his abilities and self-worth and, for the first time in his life, he found himself unable to get out of bed in the mornings. Fortunately his wife recognized the symptoms of growing depression and started calling friends they had known throughout the years.

One friend's wife related that her husband had gone through the same experience after he retired a few years earlier. "The answer for my husband," she said, "was in volunteering with a ministry that helps provide housing for the inner-city poor. The group is totally run by volunteers so there is no conflict with the founder or other leaders. My husband is able to use his military training to plan and develop an entire project himself, so he is the developer, someone else is the fund raiser, and other volunteers man the construction crews. He feels he is really contributing, and God is allowing him to use the abilities he has developed over the years to help others."

After some wise counsel from his wife, my friend found an organization that needed a first-class administrator to help schedule relief materials to their volunteer groups all over the world. He has been there for nearly ten years and plans to be there until the Lord takes him home. When he needs to, he can take off several weeks at a time to relax and travel. Since he needed to train someone to replace him in the interim, he scouted out an old Army buddy who was fed up with playing golf down in Florida and they now share the responsibilities.

*F*or you Type B personalities, . . . think out your retirement years carefully and start laying something aside before you retire, rather than trying to figure it out after you retire.

One of my most vivid examples of a classic Type B personality is Andrew, a retired fire chief from Florida.

Andrew had worked up through the ranks of his town's fire department to become the fire chief—by default. He was simply the only remaining candidate after all the others had quit in frustration because the town's mayor constantly meddled in the fire chief's business. That didn't bother Andrew at all. His personality was such that he wanted the mayor (or someone) to give him direction. At age 62 he retired, and no amount of pressure from the mayor could change his mind. Andrew had the notion that a man 62 should be able to lay back and enjoy the fruits of his labor, regardless of how small they were.

When Andrew retired he had a small pension from the public service commission, plus his Social Security of about $300 a month. This left him and his wife with a monthly shortfall of about $300 to $400, depending on some of their variable expenses. To meet this need Andrew instructed his wife (ten years his junior) that she would just have to go to work.

She had never worked during their married life and was ill-prepared for the modern work place. After several weeks of disappointment and discouragement in looking for work, she finally got a job in a small diner. Day after day she would walk to work and, after ten to twelve hours of waiting tables, would return to find Andrew awaiting his supper.

It would be easy to judge Andrew for his selfish attitude and obvious irresponsibility but, in reality, Andrew was a product of a system that convinced him to retire with little or no preparation. After having met with him several times at the request of his children, I can attest that he was a classic Type B personality. The Andrews of our society aren't particularly worried about today—or tomorrow. Type B personalities seem to get by pretty well themselves, but those who live around them are often forced to pick up the slack.

SUMMARY

For those who fit in the Type A category, the best counsel I can give is: Don't ever stop working entirely. You can slow down (and probably should) but retirement is often the first step into an early grave. Instead, plan for each phase of your life, including 65 and older. Then get involved with something that will provide the goals and rewards you need to feel that you are a productive member of society.

Most Type A personalities would be better off staying with the organization they served during their most productive years; but since many organizations require younger employees, it is sometimes necessary to step down and assume a less visible role. If your ego won't allow you to do that, you need an ego adjustment. As Proverbs 16:19 says: *"It is better to be of a humble spirit with the lowly, than to divide the spoil with the proud.*

When you approach your sixties, begin transferring some of your responsibilities to a younger person. You may find a new niche in the organization that will allow you more free time and a much longer career. The concept is entirely biblical. Jewish fathers began transferring responsibilities to their sons as they grew older so they could guide them and help ease the transfer over to the next generation.

For you Type B personalities, my best counsel is to listen to your wives who, in most marriages, are probably Type A personalities. Think out your retirement years carefully and start laying something aside before you retire, rather than trying to figure it out after you retire.

Although the temperament of Type B personalities allows them to make the transition to retirement more easily, the admonition from the Lord to remain productive still applies. Too often Type B personalities' lack of financial discipline makes them vulnerable to get-rich-quick schemes in an attempt to strike it rich. As Proverbs 23:4-5 implies: Those who attempt to get rich quickly usually end up getting poor even more quickly.

Besides, if the Lord still has work for you to do in this lifetime and you stop too early, you may find yourself working for some overbearing Type A in heaven—for the rest of eternity!

I don't think I can
overemphasize the need to
diversify your retirement funds.

Retirement Options

EARLY RETIREMENT

The option of taking early retirement can be enticing, particularly in a recession when your job may seem to be in jeopardy. But is early retirement a good idea? Let's first take a look at the early retirement option of Social Security.

Social Security offers the potential retiree the option of retiring at age 62 with reduced benefits, or continuing to work until age 65 and draw full benefits. Since this is not the chapter on Social Security benefits, I will not discuss the tests for qualifying here.

If a retiree elects to begin receiving benefits at age 62, the retirement benefits are reduced by .555 percent for each month of payout before the age of 65. For example: Let's assume you retire at age 62 (36 months before full entitlement.) Multiply 36 X .555 to get the reduction in benefits. In this case it would be 19.98 percent, so your monthly check from Social Security would be reduced by 19.98 percent when compared to what it would have been at age 65. However, it should be noted that once the early retirement election is made, it is irrevocable.

For example: Assuming that your benefits at age 65 would be $900 a month and you retired the month you turned 62, your monthly benefit would be $720.18 ($900 X 80.02 percent).

Is this early income option a financially sound idea, outside of all other considerations? To evaluate this we need to look at the all the options.

OPTION #1: INCOME FROM SOCIAL SECURITY

For the sake of discussion, I will assume our retiree has qualified for the maximum retirement benefit of approximately $1,500 per month at age 65 ($1,500 X 19.98 percent = $299.70). So the retirement check is reduced by approximately $300 a month. Or another way to say it: At $1,200 a month he receives $43,200 in benefits over the next three years.

> W hen a company offers an employee an early retirement option, it is usually to reduce the company's overhead. That . . . should tell you something.

Ignoring all other factors, such as the interest this money could earn, the time value of money, and inflation, it would take approximately 144 months (12 years) at full benefits beyond the age of 62 before the income paid during the first three years would be matched. In other words, you would have to be at least 74 years of age before any real loss occurred. Financially speaking, early retirement is a good deal under the present Social Security system.

Remember, as of 1983, those who were born after 1938 do not reach full retirement at age 65. The retirement age is gradually extended to age 67, depending on the year in which you were born. The early retirement benefits for these people will be reduced depending on what their actual maximum benefit age is. For example: Since I was born in March, 1939, my maximum benefit age is 65 years and 4 months. For someone born in 1940, it would be 65 years and 6 months.

Also bear in mind that earned income in excess of $7,080 (1991) for those under the age of 65 will reduce the monthly benefit by $1 for every $3 in "excess" income (the government's definition, not mine).

OPTION #2: COMPANY'S EARLY RETIREMENT

When a company offers an employee an early retirement option, it is usually to reduce the company's overhead. That in itself should tell you something: The benefits after retirement will be significantly less than when the retiree was fully employed.

If the retiree can take the retirement pay and move on to another job where the combination of earned income and retirement pay is greater than what he or she was making previously, it's a sound financial decision; but often that's not the case.

All too often the decision is made because it sounds like a good deal. But when the actual figures are compiled, the net result is a loss in pay. Obviously if the decision is a part of a larger plan in which other funds are available, and a subsequent career is already planned, the decision is not purely financial.

I recall a friend who had worked for the same company since graduating from high school. During that time he'd earned a college degree, and he had worked his way up in the company to head one of their major divisions. Then in the mid-eighties when the merger mania was striking corporate America, his company was absorbed through a hostile takeover. The acquisition company offered him the choice of either taking an early retirement or taking his chances in the new corporate environment.

My friend called to ask for counsel since the retirement option would reduce his income by nearly 50 percent; in addition, he really liked the job he had. I suggested that he pay to have a background check done on the principals of the take-over company through one of the companies that specialize in this area, which he did. The results were pretty conclusive: The group acquiring his company were merger specialists, noted for acquiring sound companies, stripping them of their ready assets, and then cutting them in smaller pieces for resale.

My advice was to get out while he could and take a lump sum if at all possible, which he did. The company was more than willing to give him the lump sum since he settled for less than the total of the company's contributions to his retirement plan. This allowed the company access to the residual in his account.

Within two years the takeover group had stripped the company of all the available assets, including the employees' retirement accounts. In order to gain access to the retirement funds they purchased an annuity from an affiliated insurance company. The long and the short of it was, the insurance company was just another shell owned by the same group and it filed for bankruptcy within the next five years too.

Had my friend stayed with the company, he would have been out of a job and probably would have lost the majority of his retirement benefits as well. After leaving the company, he advised many of the other employees to do the same. Most chose not to do so for the sake of their current income. Only a very few retained their jobs when the company was dissected for resale.

My friend took his lump sum and invested it (through an IRA) in high quality mutual funds. He then took his experience and used it to form a consulting company to help other takeover victims determine their best options. That work has supported him comfortably into his normal retirement age. He now works full time for the Nature Conservancy, looking for land that can be donated in trust for the benefit of future generations. For him, early retirement was a great benefit, but not for all.

A man I'll call Phil worked as the chief financial officer for a foreign furniture manufacturing company based in the U.S. The owners sold out to a Canadian company, who then changed much of the top management, including Phil's boss, the administrative vice president. His new boss quickly became his worst nightmare.

He harassed Phil about the financial reports and tried to force him to "enhance" the reports to make it easier for the company to raise capital, which Phil flatly refused to do. From that point on, Phil's life on the job was miserable.

*T*he asset [of a fixed annuity] is the guaranteed payout, which helps budget planning after retirement. The liability is . . . its inability to adjust to inflation.

Slightly more than a year after the acquisition, Phil suffered a heart attack and underwent bypass surgery. While he was recuperating, his boss took the opportunity to replace Phil with a financial officer more to his own liking. Phil still had a job, but he had no day-to-day functions. At 55 Phil was offered the "opportunity" to take early retirement. He took it.

Unfortunately, Phil made two fundamental mistakes in his retirement decision: He decided to leave his retirement funds in the company, and he accepted a monthly annuity since the benefit was higher than he could get elsewhere. After retiring, Phil retreated into a shell and withdrew from any active involvement in the business world.

When Phil had been in charge of the financial department, the employees' retirement account had been transferred to a professional investment firm, which had recommended greater diversification of the assets. Over the last ten years that Phil had worked with the company, the annual growth of the retirement account had been in excess of 15 percent under their management.

But when the new leadership took over the company, the decision was made to shift more of the retirement funds back into the parent company's stock to help finance growth internally. To insure the solvency of the plan, a high yield annuity was purchased from an insurance company in California.

At the same time all of this was occurring, Phil's health was steadily declining. Instead of exercising as he was instructed to do, he lapsed into a state of anxiety and depression—often staying in his home for days. Although Phil was a Type B personality, which is usually able to adapt, his sense of self-worth was greatly diminished. That, along with the normal post-operative depression often associated with bypass surgery, crippled him emotionally.

The best thing Phil could have done was to take his wife's advice to "go find something to do, even if it's working in a hardware store." Instead, he continued to withdraw into self-pity and depression.

In 1987 the company suffered some significant financial setbacks, and in 1988 the owners filed for bankruptcy protection. It was clear by then that the retirement fund was depleted, so the insurance company began making the annuity payments.

In 1990 the insurance company backing the plan also filed for bankruptcy protection, citing huge losses in their own junk bond portfolio. And although the state in which Phil lived had an insurance trust fund, the payout was only a fraction of the promised benefits.

But Phil never lived to see the collapse of his retirement plans because in 1989 he died of a massive heart attack. His widow told me, "Phil made a decision to die without even realizing it when he withdrew from the business world. There was just too much of himself tied up in his work to quit," she said. Once Phil left the daily routine he had loved, he simply went downhill. It is unfortunate that the same thing can be said of many early retirees (perhaps even most who are forced to retire).

OPTION #3: ANNUITY VERSUS A LUMP SUM PAYOUT

When most employees retire from a company, they are offered a variety of choices for their retirement income. Basically the options can be reduced to two: a monthly annuity or a lump sum payout. I would like to discuss these two simple, but overwhelmingly critical, choices.

The Annuity: Probably this is the least common option accepted by most retirees during the last ten years because of all the negative publicity about underfunded retirement accounts. To some extent the trend away from company-provided annuities has been good because so many of the plans have been poorly managed, especially benefit plans operated by government agencies. At least with their own money in hand, retirees are able to control their own destinies—for better or worse.

*N*ormally I advise those who are not in substantial company ownership positions to avoid the annuity option when retiring and, more specifically, the variable annuity.

Usually with a retirement plan annuity two options are given: a fixed annuity or a variable annuity. A fixed annuity means that the plan pays a fixed amount of money per month for the rest of the annuitant's life. The payout is guaranteed, irrespective of how much the plan makes or loses on its investments or what the prevailing inflation rate is.

You can probably recognize the asset and liability of a fixed annuity. The asset is the guaranteed payout, which helps budget planning after retirement. The liability is primarily its inability to adjust to inflation. The decision to receive a fixed payout must be made prior to the first month of retirement and is irrevocable.

The monthly payout from a variable annuity is adjusted, based on the actual earnings of the insurance company backing the annuity. Again, the assets and liabilities are obvious: Since the payout is adjusted according to earnings it can be a good inflation hedge, especially since inflation is a fact of life in America.

The liability is that the plan may actually lose money through bad investments, in which case your income will suffer accordingly. Even in a well-managed retirement plan, usually the investments decisions rest with the company's management, so you have little or no control over how the assets are invested. Ownership and management changeovers can adversely affect the way the plan is managed.

One of the most important decisions you will make involves the choice of a single- or two-life annuity.

Normally I advise those who are not in substantial company ownership positions to avoid the annuity option when retiring and, more specifically, the variable annuity. The exception to this rule is where the retirement account is managed by an independent group with no direct link to the parent company or organization.

If you are considering leaving your retirement funds in a company account, you need to get professional help in evaluating the way the fund is run, how it is invested, and what authority the company has in future changes to the management. The guiding rule is: When in doubt, don't!

Even if your fund is guaranteed by a major insurance company, you need to check it out carefully before deciding on your choice of an annuity or lump sum payout. An insurance company is just that: a company. Any company can fail, no matter how large it is. In my opinion, having all of your assets with a single company is too risky when looking at the future. Unless your particular plan is covered by the Pension Benefits Guaranty Corporation, an agency of the U.S. government, I suggest removing your portion if you can. You can verify if your plan is covered by contacting the office of the PBGC, 2020 K St. NW, Washington DC 20006-1860 - 202/778-8800.

As I mentioned previously, one of the most important decisions you will make involves the choice of a single- or two-life annuity. If you elect the single-life plan the payout will be higher each month, but if you die the benefits cease. Perhaps if you are a widow or widower this may not seem important at this time, but you always need to consider the future. You may get remarried, and the option to leave your annuity to your spouse would be very important. In my opinion, it is extremely rare to have a single-life plan be more beneficial in the long run. The one possible exception is when a life insurance policy can be purchased to provide for the surviving spouse at less cost per month than the two-life annuity option would be.

*M*y advice to any recent retiree is to place your retirement funds in CDs or government securities for at least one year while you make the emotional and psychological adjustment to your new way of life.

Lump Sum Option: The lump sum option is exactly what it sounds like: an option to receive your accumulated benefits in one lump sum. You then must seek out your own investments to generate the income needed.

If the funds are being distributed from a qualified pension or profit sharing plan, the proceeds must be rolled over into another tax-deferred plan within sixty days to avoid paying the taxes and premature withdrawal penalties.

For the vast majority of retirees, the best option is to roll the proceeds over into an Individual Retirement Account. If you have an existing IRA, the funds can be transferred to that account or you can establish a new IRA just for that purpose. Failure to transfer the funds into another retirement account within

sixty days of the disbursement will result in severe tax consequences, so this step is very important. You will owe a 10 percent surtax on the entire amount withdrawn, plus the federal
and state income taxes. The entire taxable amount will be
lumped on top of your income in the year of withdrawal, and
can easily push your total income into the highest tax bracket.
So, don't procrastinate!

There is a lot of misunderstanding about the use of IRAs.
An IRA is not an investment itself. It is merely a legal entity that
allows the funds to be held tax-deferred. You can have an IRA
with a mutual fund company, a stock brokerage firm, a bank,
an insurance company, or any of dozens of other authorized
institutions.

For a new retiree, one of the best options is to establish a
self-directed IRA at a local bank to hold the funds temporarily.
A self-directed IRA means that, although the funds may be temporarily deposited in the bank, you reserve the right to redirect
them at any time in the future. So upon proper notice you can
tell the bank to forward the funds to a mutual fund company,
insurance company, or any other authorized agency. This provides a way to satisfy the legal requirement of rolling the funds
into a qualified retirement account while giving you the option
later of investing the money elsewhere.

My advice to any recent retiree is to place your retirement
funds in CDs or government securities for at least one year
while you make the emotional and psychological adjustment to
your new way of life. Use that time to learn what you need to
know about retirement investing. Under no circumstances make
any financial decisions under duress, especially those based
on "hot tips." As Proverbs 24:3-4 says, *By wisdom a house is
built, and by understanding it is established; and by knowledge
the rooms are filled with all precious and pleasant riches."*

DIVERSIFICATION

I don't think I can overemphasize the need to *diversify*
your retirement funds. I will discuss some of the more practical
ways to do this later, but at this point I would like to discuss the
dangers of leaving your funds in one company's stock.

Many retirees have worked for the same company for many years—some for their entire lives. As a result, the majority of their retirement funds have been invested in their company's stock. This may or may not have been the best investment over the years, but often it was the only option provided or the company promoted it by offering matching funds in its own stock. However, after retirement the idea of leaving the majority of your assets in a single company's stock, no matter what company it is, makes no real sense.

Any company can fail, and many long-time companies do fail regularly. The economy shifts, and their area of expertise can fade. The company founder (who may have been the driving force behind the company's success) can die, and the whole nature of the company can change.

I don't care how successful your investment in a company's stock has been prior to retirement, the risk is just too great when you no longer have the income flexibility you did in earlier years.

I don't advise that you immediately go and sell all the stock you were issued. Timing in the sale of stock is often critical but, as time and the market make it possible, the ratio of one company's stock to the rest of your assets should be reduced to a level where if it dropped by 50 percent you could still maintain your lifestyle. Even then you should keep a close watch on the company and convert more if there is any significant downward trend.

I recall vividly a friend who had worked for Rich's Department Stores most of his adult life. He literally had grown up with the company as it expanded from one store in Atlanta to a sizeable chain of stores. The bulk of his net worth was held in Rich's stock, which had grown from a total investment of perhaps $25,000 to more than $600,000.

After retiring in 1980, he continued to hold the majority of his retirement income in Rich's stock, despite all of my efforts to persuade him to convert at least half of it. With the country on a "roll" in the mid-eighties, his stock continued to grow and the dividends grew accordingly. My counsel looked pretty weak then.

In 1986 Rich's sold out to the Federated Department Stores chain—a large national chain that included prestigious stores such as Bloomingdales and Macys. Unfortunately, much of Federated's expansion was accomplished with junk bond sales and, in 1990, the chain was in serious financial trouble. By 1991 they had filed for bankruptcy protection. My friend lost more than half of his total asset base before his stock could be sold—a very harsh lesson on the need to diversify.

The advice Solomon offered three thousand years ago is still just as sound today: *"Divide your portion to seven, or even to eight, for you do not know what misfortune may occur on the earth"* (Ecclesiastes 11:2).

*T*here is no substitute for knowledge when shopping for insurance; you need to know what you're looking for and what you're willing and able to afford.
The principle in insurance is: Don't pay someone else to provide what you can provide for yourself.

CHAPTER SEVEN

Insurance Decisions

This is not a discussion on whether term insurance is better than whole life, or whether a single premium plan is preferable to monthly payments. That type of information has been fully discussed in many other publications, several of which are referenced in the Appendix. Instead, what I would like to discuss is the need for insurance after retirement and some logical alternatives to the ever-rising costs.

A counselee I'll call Scott came to see me shortly after he retired from the Martin Marietta company, where he had worked as a technician for nearly thirty years.

During that time he had invested regularly in the company's employee benefits plan, into which he put 5 percent of his salary, and the company matched it with an additional 2.5 percent. During his working years this fund had grown to just over $200,000 in value. Scott elected to take his retirement as a lump sum, which he put into an IRA and invested it in CDs. That obviously was not the last word in investment planning, but it was an easily workable short-term solution.

Throughout Scott's working career his employer had provided his health insurance, life insurance, and disability insurance. A case could be made that he would no longer need the disability insurance since he would be retiring, but what about the health and life?

Scott's wife was three years younger than him, and although she worked full-time, her income would cover less than half of her actual monthly expenses in the event of Scott's death. Even after she could qualify for retirement on her own, they would not be able to live totally on retirement benefits. Scott would have to earn some income to supplement their savings and Social Security. But the immediate need was for some life insurance to bridge the gap between the time he retired and his wife turned 62.

> *T*hose whose total insurance
> needs are covered by a company
> plan should consider carrying
> another policy on their own.

I calculated that Scott would need approximately $100,000 in life insurance to adequately provide for his wife if he died. After further discussion I learned that Scott had suffered a heart attack several years earlier, and although he had no reoccurrence, he was still rated a high risk for insurance purposes. He also told me he was a mild diabetic and required periodic treatment, which certainly eliminated any chance that he would qualify for life insurance. The vast majority of companies exclude pre-existing diabetics and heart patients from their list of acceptable clients. I realized that additional life insurance was not possible.

We also examined the possibility of continuing the company-provided life insurance and found that it was not an option either. Since we had explored every life insurance alternative available and came up empty, I moved on to the next area: health insurance.

Some life insurance on Scott would have been nice, but the greater and more immediate need was for health insurance since Scott would not qualify for Medicare coverage until age 65.

We explored the prospect of getting Scott covered under his wife's company policy since it also offered a group insurance plan. Unfortunately, she lost the option to cover Scott's pre-existing conditions because he wasn't covered during the first thirty days of her employment. So that alternative was out too.

*I*t is a certainty that health care and the related costs will undergo some significant changes in the next few years.

The last possibility was that Scott could continue his company health insurance under the Comprehensive Omnibus Budget Reconciliation Act (COBRA). Under this law an employee is allowed to continue the company health insurance plan for up to eighteen months (thirty-six months in some instances) after leaving the company.

Fortunately for Scott, he was still within the option period and could continue the coverage at the employer's group insurance rate. The real shocker came when Scott heard the cost: $425 a month!

It was fortunate for Scott that they were able to obtain this coverage until he could qualify for Medicare because within a year after retirement his diabetes flared up, causing a greater problem that resulted in drug bills of nearly $500 a month, plus the doctor and hospital bills.

Scott's problems with life and health insurance could have been resolved with some preplanning. Those whose total insurance needs are covered by a company plan should consider carrying another policy on their own. Obviously, few people can afford two health policies, but Scott could have been added to his wife's plan for less than $25 a month initially. His history of diabetes would indicate the need for this precaution. The bottom line is: Think ahead. Usually once you retire it's too late to do much planning. As Proverbs 22:3 says: *"The prudent sees the evil and hides himself, but the naive go on, and are punished for it."*

HEALTH INSURANCE

Of all the potential problems facing retirees in the future, nothing looms larger than medical expenses. With the average cost of a five-day hospital bill at approximately $6,000 for relatively minor problems, these expenses can quickly plunge a retiree into long-term debt.

As I said earlier, it is a certainty that health care and the related costs will undergo some significant changes in the next few years. I wish it were possible to predict exactly what those changes will be; it would make writing this book much easier. At present, however, no one has even the slightest idea what direction health care provision will take.

The cost of providing health insurance as a retirement benefit is too expensive for most companies to justify, especially if the retiree has access to Medicare.

The possibilities range all the way from total socialization of the medical industry to requiring insurance companies to accept all applicants. In my opinion, either of these probably would raise the cost of insurance and lower the caliber of service. But most certainly, some reform must be made in Medicare.

Medicare is any insurance provider's worst nightmare; it is also any government's nightmare. Just think of the problems from the side of the insurer which, in this case, is the American taxpayer.

First, the system is designed to insure the highest risk group in America: the aged.

Second, women are a higher risk group for health care than men are—particularly older women—and a high percentage of the people on Medicare are women. *Note:* The reason older women are a higher risk group than men is because men tend not to use health services as frequently. However the high death rate among men before the age of 65 indicates that men should see a doctor more regularly.

Third, the Medicare program is administered by the least efficient sector of our economy: the federal government.

Fourth, if individuals tend to treat an insurance company's money as less precious than their own (which they do), they absolutely will devalue health care funds provided by the government.

All of these factors point to some very severe changes in the Medicare system before the turn of the century. I would like to project what I believe the minimum changes will be.

*I*nvesting in a Medicare supplemental insurance plan would be wise, even for those who have these costs paid through a company provided plan right now.

Medicare will be lumped into some form of national health care plan where only authorized doctors and hospitals will participate. This will greatly curtail services as well as costs. It may well be that government health management organizations (HMOs) will be created to treat the indigent and the aged, while private doctors and hospitals will operate on the current free market system. The model for this already exists in the form of V.A. hospitals. As one of our more lucid politicians said recently: "When you step through the door of a state-run facility, you will be facing a cadre of government bureaucrats pretending to be health care providers."

I can only guess at the direction retirees' health care will take because of the current impasse in Washington. One side stands firmly committed to a government-orchestrated plan. The other side is just as committed to a private-sector-run plan. I have therefore concluded that, in typical government fashion, we will have both. Only time will tell if this is a valid assumption.

It would also seem probable that many restrictions, or caps, will be placed on the Medicare plan, regardless of whether it is public or private. There is simply no way the Social Security system can absorb the increases that an aging population will bring. Let's pray that our society doesn't seek the less costly remedy called euthanasia.

COMPANY HEALTH PLANS

Many former executives have their health insurance benefits continued into the retirement years. There is no question that this is a great benefit in our present economy, in which the cost of health care is rising faster than almost any other commodity. There is also little doubt that many companies will be trying to drop this benefit, especially if the company is involved in a merger or buyout. Quite simply the cost of providing health insurance as a retirement benefit is too expensive for most companies to justify, especially if the retiree has access to Medicare.

Recently bankruptcy judges have tended to side with the companies that drop the health care benefits for retirees, even where a contract for these benefits exists.

I bring this up only because the few people who have this benefit should take a realistic view of the future. The trend in American business is generally down, and the trend in long-term retirement benefits is definitely down. Investing in a Medicare supplemental insurance plan would be wise, even for those who have these costs paid through a company-provided plan right now. You may not be able to qualify for the supplement later.

SUPPLEMENTAL INSURANCE (MEDIGAP INSURANCE)

Medicare is divided into two basic elements: Part A—hospitalization, and Part B—medical. Since both plans have specific stop limits and deductible amounts that the Medicare patient must absorb, many retirees have found it prudent to purchase a supplemental insurance policy to help cover these expenses. These plans are generally known as *medigap* policies. Since retirees are a large potential market for unscrupulous sales people, many worthless policies have been sold. Discerning the good from the bad is extremely important to your pocketbook.

A thorough review of the limitations of Medicare is vital to selecting the right supplemental policy.

There is no substitute for knowledge when shopping for insurance; you need to know what you're looking for and what you're willing and able to afford. The principle in insurance is: Don't pay someone else to provide what you can provide for yourself.

Covering every out-of-pocket cost is going to be very expensive—and unnecessary. What you want is a policy that will cover the major expenses that can wreck your finances at a time when you can least afford it. Since Medicare Part A and Part B cover most normal expenses, you want a policy that will cover the abnormal. For example, you may want the 20 percent deductible of Part B covered by a supplemental policy that will reimburse you on an 80/20 basis. In other words, it will pay 80 percent of the 20 percent not covered by Medicare. So your actual out-of-pocket costs are about 4 percent of what Medicare won't pay. Also, since Part A limits the number of days in the hospital that Medicare will pay, your policy should pick up that expense after Medicare stops. A single day in the hospital often runs upwards of $500. In intensive care the cost can be $2,000 a day or more. That will put a dent in most any retiree's budget.

A thorough review of the limitations of Medicare is vital to selecting the right supplemental policy. I will summarize these shortly. If you have further questions, I would recommend you purchase a copy of Faustin Jehle's book, *The Complete and Easy Guide to Social Security and Medicare,* listed in the Appendix. I believe it is the most complete and comprehensive book available on this subject.

There are several critical factors in selecting the right supplemental insurance policy, in addition to what coverage the plan offers. The best coverage in the world is useless if the company won't pay off when the need arises.

1. Always check with one or more of the insurance company rating services listed in the Appendix. Normally this is as simple as going to your local public library and looking at a current report. Some of the services will verify the rating of a company by telephone for a fee.

Verifying a company's rating over the previous three or four years is also important. A company that has been downgraded several times usually reflects a history of losses. A lower-rated company's policies may be cheaper, but its longevity may be in question.

2. Take the time to write the state insurance commissioner's office in the insurance company's home state. Ask about complaints against the company—especially failure to pay claims.

3. Carefully review the contract and particularly your right to renew in the event of claims. Sometimes low-dollar companies reserve the right to cancel your policy for excessive claims. If they have this right, your policy can be canceled at the time when you need it most.

Also verify the renewal premium clause. If the company can increase your premiums based on use, it can price you out of the market. *Note:* Although most states have specific limits on what the increases can be, this is a very difficult area to enforce. It has been my observation that by the time you get someone in the insurance commissioner's office to respond, it's too little too late.

The following is a brief summary of what Medicare A&B do not cover (at the present time). Be certain that your medigap insurance policy addresses these areas. What you don't want is a policy that only covers things like elephants falling out of trees on you.

- Medicare has a 20 percent deductible charge for hospitalization after 20 days of in-patient care.

- Medicare will not presently pay any in-hospital costs after 100 days of care.

- Medicare will not pay for nursing home care in "nonskilled nursing home facilities." Medicare pays only for skilled nursing home care. Nearly 80 percent of all nursing homes do not qualify as skilled care units.

- In-home nursing care is excluded by Medicare.

- Blood transfusions beyond the initial three pints are excluded. This is very important in operations such as bypass surgery.

- The 20 percent deductible under Medicare Plan B for doctors and medicines, as well as routine services, such as immunizations and ear and eye exams, are not covered under Medicare.

Obviously you may not wish to provide insurance for all of these excluded expenses. Total-coverage policies can often run hundreds of dollars a month. But this list will at least aid you in evaluating the various policies offered by different companies.

Note: It is illegal for anyone to knowingly sell you more than one medigap insurance policy. Usually these policies are mutually exclusive and will not pay for the same expenses. Salespeople who knowingly violate this law are subject to a $25,000 fine.

Nursing Home Insurance

With long-term care now costing from $30,000 to $60,000 a year, older persons (especially retirees) must consider how the cost of nursing home care would be funded for themselves or their loved ones. The requirement under Medicare is that the facility be a skilled care unit in order to qualify for benefits. As previously noted, only about 20 percent of all nursing care facilities in the U.S. meet this requirement.

*L*ong-term-care insurance is not for everyone. Something less than 15 percent of all retirees require a full-care facility at any time during their lives.

Medicaid, the state-run health care plan, will pay for nursing home care only in the case of indigent people. This requires that a patient's own assets (other than a home) be exhausted before the state will step in. In recent years these rules have been relaxed to allow the spouse to retain one half of the assets up to a specified amount (usually $60,000). But this exclusion varies state by state. Even under the best of circumstances this leaves very little in the way of long-term financial security for older people.

A word of spiritual admonition: Many people, Christians included, try to avoid the legal restrictions placed on Medicaid patients by transferring assets so that a family member appears to be indigent, and thus qualifies. This is unethical, as well as often illegal, not to mention very unscriptural.

There are companies that now specialize in aiding older people and their families in doing this. Remember, although the government may never detect the fraud, the Lord already has. Honesty in our society today often is deemed "not getting caught." Honesty in God's sight is doing what is right when no one else will ever know. As Joshua said, *"Choose for your-selves today whom you will serve. . .but as for me and my house, we will serve the Lord"* (24:15).

The most common ethical alternative to Medicaid at present is the purchase of an insurance policy that will pay the costs of nursing home care. Since this type of policy is relatively new, there are only a few *major* companies offering them, and the opportunity for fraud and abuse is considerable.

Long-term-care insurance is not for everyone. Something less than 15 percent of all retirees require a full-care facility at any time during their lives. With much attention focused on the financial plight of the few who need such care, it is easy to overreact. A great deal of counsel and prayer should go into this decision.

The costs of long-term-care policies are understandably expensive. The insurance companies are taking on enormous risks and ever-escalating costs. Insurance companies are in the business to make a profit, so they simply calculate the expected costs and price the policies to cover costs, plus a reasonable profit.

*Y*ou should select a company that has been in the health care business for at least twenty years.

As would be expected, the premiums on long-term-care policies increase with the age of the insured. A typical policy can cost $1,800 a year for a 65 year old person, $2,500 for a 70 year old, and $4,400 for a 75 year old, according to a 1992 report from the Seniors' Health Cooperative.

Retirees with total assets of $50,000 or less would quickly consume their asset base in annual premiums. The cumulative cost of long-term-care insurance between the ages of 65 and 75 would be something just over $30,000. Since the probability of nursing home care really begins after the age of 75, the cost of most nursing home policies escalate rapidly beyond this age. To presently provide coverage for a couple to age 75 would cost in excess of $60,000, with no assurance that the costs would not run twice that, due to inflation in the nursing home industry.

Since the Spousal Impoverishment legislation allows the non-confined spouse to retain ownership of the home, car, and other personal assets, as well as up to $62,000 in cash, the use of total-care insurance for couples with modest assets does not seem logical.

If your asset base is in excess of $100,000, excluding your home, you may want to consider this insurance. If so, there are some basic elements you will want to look for in a policy.

1. *Company stability.* Just as I mentioned earlier, if the company isn't around when you need it, you wasted your money; so verify the quality of the issuing company.

2. *Time in the business.* You should select a company that has been in the health care business for at least twenty years. Many new companies jump into a growing industry, only to withdraw later because they did not anticipate the costs. Go with a company that has been writing health care policies— especially long-term health care—for at least two decades; there aren't many. You'll find a list of some of the older companies in the Appendix.

3. *Coverage.* The policy should pay at least 80 percent of the average daily cost of a nursing home facility. Note: Often you can negotiate with a facility to accept the amount provided by the insurance policy as payment in full.

4. *Provisions.* The policy should have an automatic inflation provision to cover the increasing costs while the insured is in the care facility. Otherwise, just the inflating costs can consume all of your assets, which is precisely what you bought the policy to avoid.

5. *Payment plans.* Always take the waiver-of-premium option in a long-term-care policy. You don't want to be stuck with continuing payments that may escalate rapidly with no choice but to pay them, as would be the case if you or your spouse were in a nursing home.

SUMMARY

Long-term-care insurance is not for everyone, just as disability insurance is not for everyone. The vast majority of retirees will not need to be confined to a nursing home. For those with limited assets, the cost of protection outweighs the risk of asset depletion. For those with discretionary assets of more than $100,000, and certainly for those with assets in excess of $200,000, the cost of an insurance policy may be justified when weighed against the cost of nursing home care for several years. But pray about this decision and ask God for His wisdom. Remember what the apostle James said in James 1:5: *"But if any of you lacks wisdom, let him ask of God, who gives to all men generously and without reproach, and it will be given to him."*

*T*hose] who are not yet in their retirement years . . . need to consider carefully the need for life insurance . . . and prepare while [they're] still young.

LIFE INSURANCE

It is not uncommon for people approaching retirement age to suddenly realize that after they retire they will still need some life insurance. If you're still healthy, the situation is not so critical. However, if you have any pre-existing conditions, you'll probably either be rated in a higher risk category or denied coverage altogether. Unfortunately, there is very little that can be done if you are not insurable, so I'll concentrate on the options available to those who are.

For those who are not yet in their retirement years, I would counsel that you need to consider carefully the need for

life insurance in your sixties and seventies (or older) and prepare while you're still young.

TERM OR WHOLE LIFE

No insurance, term or whole life, is going to be inexpensive for people in their sixties or older. All insurance companies operate from actuarial tables that predict the probabilities
of death, and it is a fact that the older we get, the closer to
death we get.

*N*o one insurance plan fits
every person or situation, regardless of what any whole life or
term salesperson says.

Those who purchased whole life insurance in their
younger years are paying less for it in their later years only because they have paid for a longer period of time. Meanwhile the
insurance companies have had the use of their excess premiums for that period of time. But for those who are in need of
additional coverage, the decision is: Should you buy term or
whole life beyond the age of 60?

The same general principles apply at 60 plus that applied
at age 30.

Term insurance (at any age) initially is cheaper than policies that build cash reserves. Quite simply, term is cheaper because you "rent" the coverage based on your current age. The
cash value policy must average the cost per year over your total
life expectancy.

Let me use a simplistic example. Let's assume a 65 year
old man wants to buy a $10,000 whole life policy and his life
expectancy is nine years. The insurance company estimates
what it can earn on his premiums for the next nine years and

prices the policy accordingly. For the sake of discussion, let's assume the total premium is $8,000, or $800 a year.

But since the risk goes up as the insured ages, this person might be able to buy a one year (annual) term policy at age 65 for $400. The next year, however, the rate would increase to reflect his increased age and might cost $450; the next year it would be $500, and so on until, by age 70, he would be paying $1,500 a year. (**The amounts used are illustrative, not actual.**)

If the need for insurance is temporary, such as providing a bridge policy until his wife is 65 (in three years), then the term plan would serve his needs best. If the need for insurance exists for the rest of his life, he would be better served with the whole life plan. No one insurance plan fits every person or situation, regardless of what any whole life or term salesperson says.

In order to buy the correct policy you must first determine your needs. Then contact at least two independent agents who sell both term and whole life and have them present the cost breakdown of their best products. Personally I would also check the annual insurance edition of *Consumers Reports* magazine to verify which companies are rated the best in terms of cost and financial solvency. And as previously recommended, verify the rating of any company you plan to use through one of the national rating services listed in the Appendix.

TELEVISION POLICIES

I'm often asked about the value of life insurance policies sold by celebrities on television. In large part, these are middle-of-the-road term policies. They are neither better nor worse than many products sold by local agents; they are only marketed better.

One principle you always need to bear in mind is: There is no free lunch when it comes to buying insurance. Many of these plans advertise "You can't be turned down—for any reason." The way the company can offer this guarantee is by requiring a two-year exclusion period during which the policy will not pay (this eliminates most terminally ill clients). The policies are usually higher in cost than those available through a local agent, and they either escalate in cost or decline in face value. In general, you will do better with a local agent.

CANCER POLICIES

The threat of cancer, and its related medical costs, has given rise to special insurance policies commonly called cancer policies. These policies are normally sold as riders (or supplemental plans) to your normal health insurance plan, including Medicare. Normally they are very specific in their coverage and, in fact, this is perhaps their greatest limitation.

*A*s a general rule, those facing retirement do not need disability insurance since their incomes will be independent of a regular job [though they may need a] disability policy to provide some "gap" coverage until [they] qualify for Social Security benefits.

There is not just one type of cancer, but rather many varieties—all the way from leukemia to epidermal melanoma (skin cancer). If you elect to purchase a cancer policy you need to be sure that the wording in your contract is broad enough to cover any type of cancer treatment.

Virtually no insurance policy will provide for treatments not approved by the American Medical Association (AMA). This includes a variety of herbal and vitamin therapies used in other countries, generally by non-licensed practitioners.

In general, the insurance agents I consulted advise against cancer policies, except in instances where clients have a high incidence of cancer in their immediate families. Obviously the insurance companies also realize their exposure is higher in such cases, so they will either charge a higher fee or deny coverage based on family history.

DISABILITY INSURANCE

As a general rule, those facing retirement do not need disability insurance since their incomes will be independent of a regular job. However, in one of the earlier examples the wage earner had the need for a disability policy to provide some "gap" coverage until he could qualify for Social Security bene fits.

If you feel the need for disability insurance, a few simple rules may help you make the right choice.

1. Look for a plan that satisfies your precise need. If you only need coverage for three or four years, the policy should be a term plan with a fixed cost per year.

2. Most disability policies will exclude pre-existing conditions for at least one to two years (except for non-qualifying group plans). This is usually true even if your pre-existing condition occurred several years earlier. So be certain what is covered and what is excluded before you pay your first premium. There is absolutely no substitute for reading and understanding the policy. The insurance company is bound only by the terms of your written contract, not by what your agent tells you.

3. Check the quality of your policy (and company) with an independent source. I usually recommend the annual insurance report from *Consumer Reports* magazine. Most public libraries will have a copy on file.

OTHER INSURANCE NEEDS

Your need for home, auto, and other types of insurance do not normally change as a result of retirement, unless your lifestyle changes drastically. Therefore your coverage also will not change significantly. About the only recommendation I can make is to investigate alternative sources of insurance, such as the American Association of Retired Persons (AARP), or the Government Employees' Insurance Company (GEICO). GEICO is one of several preferred companies for auto, home, and life insurance. Both are listed in the Appendix.

*B*e certain that you carry
adequate liability limits on all
of your home and auto policies.

These are available to you before retirement, but if you are retired, often the rates will drop accordingly. Most retirees are better risks because they stay at home more, and are not involved in rush hour traffic on a daily basis. One additional bit of information is necessary: Because you are facing retirement, your attitude needs to be one of preservation of capital. A major lawsuit can strip you of assets at a time when they cannot be replaced. Be certain that you carry adequate liability limits on all of your home and auto policies. I would suggest also that you carry an umbrella policy that will extend your liability limits to $1 million or more. If you use the same company for both your home and auto insurance, you can usually purchase an umbrella policy for a very reasonable fee in most areas of the country. Failure to carry adequate liability insurance in our litigating society is "penny wise and pound foolish," in my opinion.

Alternatives to Insurance

For those who cannot acquire insurance, or cannot afford it, there are ways to reduce some of the after-death costs—specifically burial expenses. With the cost of a basic funeral running $4,000 to $6,000, it is good stewardship to plan ahead. Too often even Christians avoid planning in this area because they don't want to face the realities of dying. As best I know, dying is not an option for any of us, and planning can greatly reduce the financial and emotional burden on your loved ones.

There are two alternatives to costly funeral expenses for most of us: joining a memorial society, or prepaying the funeral expenses.

The Memorial Society is a nationwide, nonprofit organization that specializes in low-cost funeral arrangements. I belong to the Georgia Memorial Society chapter, which is a part of the national group. By joining the society and prepaying a small fee ($25) I am then guaranteed a greatly reduced funeral at participating funeral homes. At present the cost of a funeral through the society is approximately $600. You can contact one of the Society's affiliates in your state by looking under "Memorial Societies" in your telephone business directory.

There are some restrictions associated with this type of service, including transportation and the cost of caskets. But for those who don't desire an elaborate funeral, it is an excellent option.

A national service, such as the Memorial Society, simply pre-arranges for basic burial costs at a reduced rate. You can prearrange funeral and burial services with most local funeral homes, if you desire. By doing so in advance the costs are usually greatly reduced. The average cost in a pre-arranged funeral is often half of what it would be if contracted immediately after death. You might logically ask, "Why not join the Memorial Society and further reduce the costs?" The reason is the Memorial Society has a limited number of participating funeral homes. You may choose to use one closer to your residence.

One significant benefit of pre-arranged funerals is that family members are saved the emotional grief of dealing with these issues immediately after the death of a loved one.

If you elect to prearrange for a funeral, be sure that the funds are kept in an escrow account by the funeral home. I have counseled many couples who prepaid for such expenses, only to discover that the funeral home spent the money and later went out of business—in which case the clients lost their money.

USE OF A CAFETERIA PLAN

If you decide to work part time after retirement, either for another company or for yourself, there is an opportunity worth investigating: the 125 plan (often called a Cafeteria Plan).

A Section 125 (IRS code identification) allows employees to have a portion of their incomes (up to 100 percent) directed to a tax exempt fund in which the proceeds can be used to pay for medical, dental, optical, and other related expenses.

This means that if you work for a company (your own or otherwise), you can designate up to *100 percent* of your income into an account excluded from federal, state, and FICA taxes, provided those funds are used only to pay for medical expenses. These funds will not effect your qualification for Social Security benefits since they will not be reported as earned income.

If you decide to start your own corporation after retiring, you can establish a 125 plan of your own. I recommend that you contact an advisory group specializing in these plans to assist in the details. The paperwork is relatively uncomplicated and well within the capabilities of most people to administer with little help. A list of some companies that handle these accounts is provided in the Appendix.

The only prohibition on the use of 125 funds is that *all* allocated funds must be used each year or they revert to the parent company. That will not represent a problem if you also own the company; if you don't, you'll need to be sure you allocated approximately what you know you will be able to utilize.

I know several retirees who utilize the 125 plan to pay for virtually all of their non-reimbursed medical expenses. One of my neighbors works ten hours a week for a company and assigns all of his income to the 125 account. It's a good deal for both sides since he uses the funds to pay for all of his and his wife's medical expenses, and the company doesn't have to pay FICA or worker's compensation on his wages.

*R*etirees are a formidable group, and many more services are opening up to meet their needs. Usually these are volunteer organizations manned by the older people who want to stay active—a concept I heartily support (as does God's Word).

CHAPTER EIGHT

Reducing Overhead in Retirement

During the sixties and seventies most Americans thought of retirees as the old people who are no longer a part of the system, but that's no longer true. Americans over age 60 are now the largest voting block in the nation, representing nearly one out of every four registered voters. They also dominate the thinking of most politicians in our country simply because, unlike many others, they *do* vote.

Many industries now specifically target their products to this group of older Americans. They may not be the biggest buyers of durable goods such as refrigerators, washing machines, or sports cars (like the younger generations are) but they dominate the travel, health, and investment industry's lists of top clients.

In many ways older Americans today are doing a disservice to the younger generations. They have more time and often more money to support the causes that benefit them directly. Too often this means placing more of the financial burden on the working group of younger Americans to support programs aimed solely at helping retirees, such as Medicare. I don't mean to imply that retirees shouldn't have adequate health care provided, but they must also consider the economic impact these programs have on our economy and be willing to bear a larger portion of the costs themselves. Some can't, but many can.

As our economy runs out of options to fund programs for retirees, we will almost certainly see changes like "means testing" applied to Medicare and perhaps to retirement benefits. Many retirees argue that they paid for their benefits in their working careers but, for many, the benefits of programs like Medicare didn't even exist when they were contributing.

Be that as it may, retirees are a formidable group, and many more services are opening up to meet their needs. Usually these are volunteer organizations manned by the older people who want to stay active—a concept I heartily support (as does God's Word).

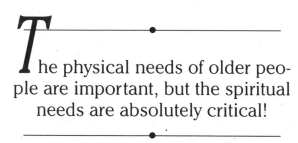

*T*he physical needs of older people are important, but the spiritual needs are absolutely critical!

I would like to mention a few organizations that operate on a national level to help older people. Some of the services are oriented to those who lack the resources to pay for the help they need. Others are available to anyone.

MEALS ON WHEELS

Not long ago my own mother suffered a broken pelvis as a result of a fall. Since she was unable to take care of herself for a period of time, a group in her community known as Meals on Wheels brought her hot meals daily. They provided enough so that my stepfather could save some from the noon meal for their evening meal. This, along with the help my sister provided in the evenings, kept her well fed (malnutrition is one of the biggest problems with shut-ins).

If we had been paying for the service that Meals on Wheels provided, it would have cost several hundred dollars a month. Since we could pay something, we donated the cost of the food and gas for the vehicles to help someone else. All of the labor involved in Meals on Wheels is provided by volunteers who take turns helping those who cannot help themselves.

There are many such service organizations available in almost every community. I heartily encourage you to make contact with them, support them financially, and donate some time if you can. (See "Programs for Older People" in the Appendix.)

CHURCH HELP

I wish that more older Christians would get involved in the lives of retirees outside of their own churches. The ministry that can be accomplished by showing concern for the physical needs of retirees is demonstrable in any church that takes the time to do it.

The physical needs of older people are important, but the spiritual needs are absolutely critical! When we help someone in the name of the Lord, it often opens the door to sharing the message of salvation. That will last for an eternity. Too often we are so busy in the church we neglect the opportunity to reach the unsaved. In Matthew 25 the Lord equated meeting physical needs with spiritual commitment. His words are a strong admonition to help others in need. *"And the King will answer and say to them, 'Truly I say to you, to the extent that you did it to one of these brothers of Mine, even the least of them, you did it to Me'"* (Matthew 25:40).

I have been to a church in the Northeast that takes James's instructions as a command, *"If a brother or sister is without clothing and in need of daily food, and one of you says to them, 'Go in peace, be warmed and be filled,' and yet you do not give them what is necessary for their body, what use is that?"* (James 2:15-16). If I understand correctly what this says, we are to be involved in the physical needs of those around us; this church I mentioned does just that.

Several years ago the pastor was confronted with a situation that ultimately led to a new church ministry. A woman from his congregation had been preparing meals for some elderly people living near her home. She had learned of their needs from her daughter, who worked at the county health clinic.

Too often we think that any program, to be effective, somehow has to be linked to government aid or at least done on a large scale.

Often friends would bring these older people to the clinic for treatment. The most common ailment the doctors at the clinic had to deal with was malnutrition. Usually those who were malnourished lived by themselves and either lacked the funds to buy adequate food, or they lacked the physical ability to prepare it. The county had no facility to provide meals for shut-ins. This lady took it upon herself to begin a home food service, providing meals at least once a day for six older people.

She came to the pastor after her ministry had grown to the point that she could no longer do it out of her home—both in time and costs. She asked the pastor if she could use the church's kitchen facility during the week when it was idle. The pastor not only agreed, he also preached a sermon on the principle of being a servant to others and challenged his congregation to get involved.

As a result of this rather meager beginning, this church has developed a county-wide program to help older retirees in their community. They minister to more than 100 elderly shut-ins every day.

The church has one group that prepares and delivers the food; another provides in-home health services for those who are injured or bedridden. Another group does home cleaning and minor repair work. The purpose is to help meet the physical needs of these neighbors, but the greater goal is to meet their spiritual needs as well.

Too often we think that any program, to be effective, somehow has to be linked to government aid or at least done on a large scale. That simply is not so. Virtually every program from the Salvation Army to the Red Cross was begun by the efforts of one person. Get involved in your own community.

THE AMERICAN ASSOCIATION OF RETIRED PERSONS (AARP)

Most Americans are familiar with the AARP. If you have stayed in a motel in the last ten years, you've probably been asked if you are a member of the AARP. If you're more than 50, the motel usually offers a reduced rate. The same is true of many restaurants and other establishments.

The AARP was founded in 1963 by retired teacher Dr. Ethel Percy Andrus in Los Angeles and now has over thirty-one million members. The political clout of the AARP members can be felt in any legislation effecting older people that comes up before the Congress. I guess the term "older" is relative anymore since the AARP accepts anyone 50 or older for membership.

The list of products and services available to AARP members fills a sixty-four page catalog the association publishes. The benefits range from information on housing and automobiles to preparing income taxes. There are some 3,600 chapters of the AARP around the country, utilizing nearly 500,000 volunteers to do everything from election campaigning to seminars on how to budget in retirement (a good idea).

In selecting the insurance plan you need for health, life, or nursing homes, the AARP has an assortment of informative brochures for little or no cost. After having reviewed much of the information the association provides, I found the services to be extremely helpful and reasonably priced.

The balance on the other side is that too often the AARP seeks an agenda contrary to the best interests of the younger generation. Unless the costs of Social Security and Medicare can be brought under control, the workers of the early twenty-first century will be paying 40 percent or more of their incomes to support it.

Obviously few people, young or old, want to see the system modified to the point that current retirees are put out of the system, but some compromise is necessary. There is absolutely no way that the automatic cost-of-living increases can be maintained without destroying the financial lives of young families.

I say this to encourage you to take a reasonable stand as a current or prospective retiree. Think about the well-being of the entire country, not just retirees.

COUNTY SERVICES

A system of local community help exists outside of Medicare and Medicaid that has been around a lot longer than either of those programs. In some communities it is called community services and includes health clinics that administer minimal health services, transportation for those who cannot drive themselves, and even emergency help for bedridden patients.

In our community the county operates a fleet of vans that pick up and deliver older people to the doctor, library, grocery stores, and other locations where they can help themselves. They administer flu shots for the elderly (and young), as well as help to organize retirees to speak to public schools as experts on a variety of topics.

A check of the yellow pages in your area will help you to locate these services. If you don't presently have a need for the help they offer, perhaps you will be able to help them do their jobs by volunteering some time.

THE ADVANTAGE OF LOCATION

Just as it is easier to rent a boat in an area with lots of water, so too it's easier to locate retirement services in an area with lots of retirees. The principle is really pretty simple: If you need help after retirement, go to a place that has plenty of retirees—such as Arizona, California, or Florida.

Having grown up in Florida, I can attest to the fact that many of the services offered are geared to retirees and their lower incomes. Obviously there are exceptions, such as West Palm Beach where the more wealthy retirees locate. In these areas it is actually harder to live on a modest retirement income because the wealthier retirees have so much to spend that they bid up the services (as well as the tax base and property values). But as you move up the state into areas such as Sarasota, Bradenton, and Leesburg, you'll find more modest income retirees.

*I*f your lifestyle allows you to relocate, or live in a non–income-tax state for at least six months a year, it can save you some money.

In these areas it is possible to live on less because the services are oriented to lower incomes; and when you locate around people of like means, the pressure to compete is lessened somewhat. For instance, although it's not fashionable to live in a mobile home in West Palm Beach, in Leesburg it's both fashionable and normal; the community abounds with them. For retirees who have sold their more expensive homes in other areas, buying a mobile home and investing the residual can greatly enhance their retirement years. And, contrary to popular opinion, mobile homes do not attract tornadoes. It's just that when a park is hit by a tornado the damage is severe and attracts a lot of media attention.

Many states have purposely tried to attract retirees through lower state taxes, including income, real estate, and inheritance taxes. Since the tax base in an area can be of great importance to retirees who can live wherever they want, I would like to focus on this subject for a moment.

Income taxes. At present there are eight states that have no personal income tax: Florida, Tennessee, Alaska, Nevada,

South Dakota, Texas, Washington, and Wyoming. If you live in a state that does assess state income taxes, you know what an overhead this can be on a fixed income.

The legalities of establishing residency in any state normally requires living there six months and a day, plus being a registered voter in that state. If your lifestyle allows you to relocate, or live in a non-income-tax state for at least six months a year, it can save you some money.

State Inheritance Taxes. An additional consideration is the tax a state levies on your assets at death. In general, most states allow the same exemptions the federal tax codes provide, so estates of $600,000 or less are exempt. But the states that don't make this allowance can take a sizeable portion of your estate assets. The following chart shows how the various states treat assets upon the owner's death.

As you can see, choosing the state of residence in which you plan to live out your life can be of benefit to your heirs. At present, the states of Massachusetts, Louisiana, New York, Ohio, Pennsylvania, and Rhode Island are the worst for estate taxes since they also tax the spouse's portion of the estate.

*I*f you use a buying club
properly . . . it can save
you a great deal of money on
products you normally buy.

In addition to inheritance taxes, many states also have fees for probating a will that can run into the thousands of dollars. Check with the office of the Probate Court in your county to verify what the costs are where you live. Good estate planning can help to reduce or eliminate these expenses. You will find more information on this topic in the chapter on estate planning.

State Inheritance Taxes

State	Death tax ($) On $600,000 estate left to: Spouse	Child	State	Death tax ($) On $600,000 estate left to: Spouse	Child
Alabama	None	None	Montana	0	0
Arizona	None	None	Nebraska	0	5,850
Arkansas	None	None	Nevada	None	None
California	None	None	New Hampshire	0	0
Colorado	None	None	New Jersey	0	0
Connecticut	$0	$37,875	New Mexico	None	None
Delaware	0	31,250	New York	25,500	25,500
Dist. of Columbia	None	None	North Carolina	0	7,000
Florida	None	None	North Dakota	None	None
Georgia	None	None	Ohio	$2,100	$30,100
Hawaii	None	None	Oklahoma	0	17,725
Idaho	None	None	Oregon	None	None
Illinois	None	None	Pennsylvania	36,000	36,000
Indiana	0	24,950	Rhode Island	7,900	12,400
Iowa	0	39,825	South Carolina	0	33,000
Kansas	0	21,750	South Dakota	0	41,250
Kentucky	0	45,370	Tennessee	0	0
Louisiana	$17,050	$17,050	Texas	None	None
Maine	None	None	Utah	None	None
Maryland	6,000	6,000	Vermont	None	None
Massachusetts	23,500	55,500	Virginia	None	None
Michigan	0	33,700	Washington	None	None
Minnesota	None	None	West Virginia	None	None
Mississippi	0	1,400	Wisconsin	0	56,250
Missouri	None	None	Wyoming	None	None

BUYING CLUBS

One great advantage a retiree has over most people who work full-time jobs is time! If you'll take advantage of this asset you can extract some significant savings. Ordinarily I don't recommend buying clubs because the majority of people who join them do so impulsively. Most of them end up ordering things they wouldn't buy ordinarily and, although they actually do save money on the purchases they make, it still costs them more in the long run. The majority of people who join a buying club stop using it within a few months and, consequently, they waste the money they spent on membership fees.

If you use a buying club properly, however, it can save you a great deal of money on products you normally buy. The clubs that I have investigated and feel are of good quality are listed in the Appendix. This is by no means a complete list, and I'm sure I probably have left out someone's good plan, but I can only comment on plans I know. I could not possibly check out all the plans in existence.

The one feature most of the newer buying clubs offer, which I believe makes them viable, is the ability to ship products directly to your home via one of the parcel services. By utilizing home delivery you can buy nonperishable food goods, garden supplies, household supplies, and other items. If you happen to wear a standard clothing size, you may even find it worthwhile to purchase your clothes this way.

Not only are the prices generally lower from a good buying club but, as of this date, the items purchased out of state are not subject to state sales taxes.

If you're an average-income retiree, a buying club should be able to save you as much as 35 percent on your cost of food, clothes, medicines, household goods, and the like. This translates to about $2,500 a year in savings. Obviously this also means that discipline must be applied to all spending or the savings can quickly be consumed in unnecessary purchases. In other words, you have to live on a *budget* to exact any real savings from a buying club, or any other cost savings idea.

Bartering

An extension of using your best asset (time) is to barter your time for someone else's goods or services. Most Americans do not engage in bartering simply because working Americans have more money than time. This lack of time and availability of money have given rise to the fast food business and to pre-pared foods. Although these are convenient, they come at a high cost because the buyers are paying others for their labor. As a retiree you can reverse this trend to your own advantage.

I need to emphasize something here: Bartering is *not* an unrealistic concept suitable only for big companies. Few people realize how much bartering takes place naturally in our economy. In the past I have traded counseling services for dental work and books for advertising space. In the business world, such transactions are done regularly. I have a friend who races cars for a living. He regularly trades his promotional abilities for automobiles and other necessities. These are all taxable transactions but usually the taxes amount to less than 40 percent of the value of the products.

As a retiree, you have the time to seek out barters that will benefit both you and the other party. For example, let's assume that your dentist has a child who needs tutoring in math and you're a retired math teacher. The two needs make a perfect match.

Or suppose you visit your friendly family physician and notice that his office could use some painting or redecorating. If you have the time and talent, a deal can be struck that will benefit you both.

I know a retired painter who virtually never pays cash for any dental, medical, or legal work. He simply offers his services to the practitioners who usually have more money than time and are desperate for anyone reliable to do some work around their homes and offices. Ask your dentist or doctor if you don't believe it.

I also know a retiree who offers to baby-sit for her dentist in exchange for his services. Not only does she save the money she would otherwise have to pay for dental care, but she gets about twice the equivalent hourly baby-sitting rate she would if the dentist were having to pay in cash also. Everyone benefits from bartering.

My stepfather took up golf after retiring and became an ardent golf fan. But since he is a retired Navy chief living on a modest retirement income in Florida, the cost of golfing very often is beyond his budget. He has found a way to reduce the costs by offering his services to some pro shops in exchange for green's fees on slack days. It has turned out to be a good arrangement for both since he is a good salesman, and he makes friends quickly.

I particularly like bartering because both parties feel like they get a good deal. In cash transactions, often people will feel cheated; especially if they discover they paid too much, or charged too little. But in a barter situation, you get what you want and the other person gets what he or she wants. So usually both are happy.

I don't generally recommend joining a barter club, however. These clubs exchange goods and services between various groups of people and take a percentage of each transaction. So if you wanted to exchange your time (say painting) you would receive credits that could be used to buy other goods or services you need.

In theory this sounds great; but in practice, most of the barter clubs don't have a wide enough membership to provide the normal products and services most people want. So you end up giving more than you get. Even worse, most of the barter clubs I have known about have gone out of business, leaving many people with nothing to show for their efforts.

If you decide to try bartering, which I heartily recommend, consult with a good accountant in your area about the taxability of the exchanges. As of this date the IRS generally treats any barter as taxable. Remember that your relationship to the Lord is far more important than the small amount of tax that you might save by cheating. As Isaiah 59:2 says, *"But your iniquities have made a separation between you and your God, and your sins have hidden His face from you, so that He does not hear."*

*T*ake at least one year
after retiring before you make
any relocation decisions.

Where to Retire

In the last chapter I discussed briefly some thoughts about where to retire, but I decided that this issue is important enough to warrant more attention.

If you have a choice of where to locate after retirement, it is important to think through your decision very carefully. I have known many retirees over the years who chose to relocate for a variety of reasons. Some made the right decisions about relocating and loved it. Others made the wrong decisions and lived to regret it, as well as spending a lot of money to correct their errors. There are several important factors involved in deciding where to live after retirement. Some are purely financial and thus quantitative; those I can help you with. But others are emotional and thus qualitative; these require a time of dedicated prayer and are outside of my circle of influence. Whatever you do, don't act hastily or you'll almost certainly live to regret it.

There are three big DON'Ts when it comes to the decision about where to live after retirement.

1. *Don't act out of emotion.* The same mentality that tempts people on vacation to buy into a time-share condo they'll probably never use causes many retirees to rush to Florida, Colorado, or Arizona. It's called *impulse*.

2. *Don't make a hasty decision.* Making quick decisions about anything will get you in trouble most of the time; you can't really trust your feelings. The feeling you get when visiting friends in Florida may make their lives seem idyllic. And perhaps (in a very few instances) life is ideal for them in Florida. But that does not mean the southern climate will suit your temperament. Take at least one year after retiring before you make any relocation decisions.

3. *Don't think you can escape from the real world.* The pace in most retirement communities is decidedly slower than in most other areas. Usually time is counted on a daily basis rather than hourly. For many people this suits their personalities and they adapt well. But for many new retirees this can often seem like stepping into a geriatric care center. You'll also find that people living in retirement communities have the same problems as everyone else.

Maintaining a Second Home

It's possible that if you have lived all of your life in a cold climate, you long for the warm rays of the Florida sun. But along with the climate comes a proliferation of insect life, bland seasons, and high air conditioning bills. If you're used to a change of season in the fall, as many northerners are, you may find the climate in Florida or Arizona too much of the same all year long.

For some people the balance has been found by maintaining homes in different areas. But for most retirees that is unrealistic for their budgets. Many retirees I have counseled who tried maintaining multiple residences in spite of their limited finances ended up in trouble, and then they couldn't enjoy either place.

The average cost of maintaining a second home, even one that is totally debt-free, is not less than $3,000 a year, and can often run twice that in many areas. If the property is worth $50,000, the loss of earnings on that money makes the real cost more like $10,000 a year!

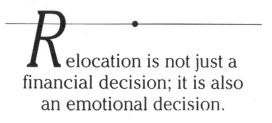

Relocation is not just a financial decision; it is also an emotional decision.

If you feel that you would like to retire in another state, take at least one year to evaluate it carefully. The rent you pay for a year may be the best money you will ever spend—especially when compared to the cost of moving your belongings across several states and then moving them back again.

FAMILY TIES

If you live close to your children and grandchildren, it's important to assess the emotional effects of moving several states away, even if the lower living costs justify it. I have known many retirees who moved to a state that offered better retirement benefits, only to sell out in a year or two and move back to their home state. Relocation is not just a financial decision; it is also an emotional decision that both husband and wife must pray about before reaching any conclusions.

EMPLOYMENT

If after retiring you decide to relocate in an area saturated with retirees and you need to earn some part-time income, you may find yourself in competition with a lot of other retirees. Usually the job market in these areas is pretty slim. In most instances your best opportunity for employment lies much closer to home.

Most people spend the majority of their lives building relationships in the area where they live and work. These can be essential after retiring if you need extra income. If you have a skill or trade that is marketable anywhere, location probably won't affect you. But in the next decade a retiree who needs to work part time will be the norm, not the exception, in my opinion. So think about how and where you might work and investigate the possibilities thoroughly before selecting a new location.

OTHER TAXES

I mentioned earlier that several states have no personal income taxes, but there are other taxes to consider, not the least of which are real estate taxes. If you decide to move to another state, carefully study the property tax rates—both county and city. In addition, you need to be conscious of recent trends (especially growth trends) where you locate.

Usually in retirement areas the older people have enough political clout to keep real estate taxes down. Increasingly high taxes can make it virtually impossible for a retiree to maintain a reasonable standard of living.

*O*ne of the major issues of the nineties will be safety and security for older Americans.

I have a friend who relocated from Ohio to Gwinett County, Georgia, after selling his business. He chose the North Georgia area because of its moderate but seasonal climate and relatively mild winters (compared to Ohio at least). He also liked the somewhat rural atmosphere, low home prices, and low property taxes.

After selling his home in Ohio, he and his wife were able to purchase an equivalent home in Lawrenceville, Georgia, for about half of what they sold their home for, leaving them more money to invest for retirement income.

What they didn't know in 1976 was that Gwinett County would become the fastest growing county in the U.S. by 1980. As a result of this growth, county services were greatly strained and property taxes had to be increased dramatically. Within five years of moving to Georgia, his property taxes were increased by more than 800 percent! Granted, his property value went up as well, but since he had no intention of selling, this was of small consolation.

Had he chosen a more developed area with many more retirees, they might have banded together to help control the escalation in taxes; unfortunately there were too few retirees in his area to influence the local politicians.

In 1983 he was forced to sell his home and relocate again to another small town—Clayton, Georgia—where he now lives. Since the 1986 Tax Reform Act shut down much of the real estate development in Georgia, he hopes to remain where he is for a long while. If his taxes continue to increase as the state's need for more revenue seems to dictate, he may once again be forced to relocate. "If so," he says, "next time I'll flock in with some other old 'buzzards' who can pressure the politicians not to tax us out of our homes" (an important consideration).

Keep Your Options Open

If you have not yet retired, you need to give some careful consideration to where you intend to spend your retirement years. As you have the opportunity to travel and talk with others, ask some questions pertinent to your future decision:

- What is the weather like?
- What about utility rates?
- What about hospital accessibility and rates?
- What about the availability of geriatric physicians?
- What about real estate taxes?
- What about income taxes?
- What about personal property taxes?
- What about the crime rate?

A negative response on any two or more of these issues should cause you to reevaluate that area as your future retirement location.

One of the major issues of the nineties will be safety and security for older Americans. Crime in the major metropolitan areas is getting worse all the time, and there would appear to be no slackening in sight (short of a spiritual revival). Any retiree would be wise to take this into consideration—especially in areas where major industries are shutting down. God may be calling you to minister in these areas, in which case you should stay there, by all means. But otherwise it may be to your advantage (and safety) to move to a more rural area.

The number of organizations dedicated to improving the overall quality of life for older people has grown from a few to many dozens. A list providing an overview of some of these groups is in the Appendix.

*T*he key to any successful investment strategy is twofold: Be knowledgeable enough to make the most
of your own decisions, and diversify
to the highest degree possible with
the funds you have available.

CHAPTER TEN

Investment Ideas for Retirees

Since I have written a book specifically on investing *(Investing for the Future,* Victor Books, 1992), I pondered how much investment information to include in this book on retirement. I decided that if I didn't include any information here then those who bought this book might feel they were slighted, since investing is such an important part of retirement decisions. But, on the other hand, if I occupied too much space in this book, those who bought *Investing for the Future* would feel like they had paid for the same information twice.

I resolved my dilemma by rereading the investment book. I realized that when I wrote it I had not covered thoroughly the area of retirees' investing, since the book was meant to cover people from 20 to 60 plus years of age. Had I attempted to discuss retirees' investing, that book would have been closer to 400 pages in length instead of 260 pages.

What I will try to do here is concentrate only on the 60-plus age group investment strategy. If you're in a younger age range, I would encourage you to get a copy of the earlier book and review the strategy that fits your age range and long-term objectives.

In that earlier work I outlined three basic seasons of life:

1. 20 to 40 years of age
   For this age group the strategy should be to determine a reasonable lifestyle and control spending to free a monthly surplus.
2. 40 to 60 years of age
   The strategy in this age range should be to retire all debts, including the home mortgage, and invest in high growth areas.
3. 60 years of age and older
   The strategy for this age group is to settle on a retirement lifestyle and preserve assets in reasonably secure investments.

Now to expand this last group further, I would like to discuss investment strategy for three asset groups: $10,000 to $50,000; $50,000 to $100,000; $100,000 or more to invest.

MODEST INVESTMENT RESOURCES: $10,000 TO $50,000

To those who have struggled to save during their working careers, $50,000 or even $15,000 may not seem modest but, in investment terms, it is. Anyone beyond the age of 60 needs to develop a more conservative philosophy about investing, but those with limited assets must go beyond conservative; they must be cautious!

If all of your income needs are provided through retirement annuities, your cash surplus is probably available for traveling—or whatever you desire. But since this is usually not the case, the income from your savings will need to be maximized, while assuming the least risk possible.

MUTUAL FUNDS

The key to any successful investment strategy is twofold: Be knowledgeable enough to make the most of your own decisions, and diversify to the highest degree possible with the funds you have available.

With $50,000 or less I normally recommend investing primarily in balanced mutual funds. These funds will provide the highest degree of diversification and expert management while yielding the highest return (normally). Obviously, if you already have some other investments, such as rental properties that have done well for you, it would be wise to keep them. Basically I'm referring to new investments made after age 60.

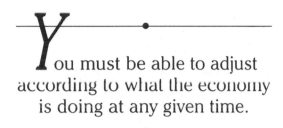

Y ou must be able to adjust according to what the economy is doing at any given time.

Within most mutual fund companies there are a variety of "families" or different kinds of funds from which to choose. These range from funds made up of government securities to utility company stocks (and bonds), common stocks, municipal bonds, and any number of other products—depending on the specialty of the mutual fund company.

Usually you can switch between any of the funds offered by a company with little or no cost involved. I believe this is an essential prerequisite to selecting a fund because no investment can be stagnant and survive in the coming economy, in my opinion. You must be able to adjust according to what the economy is doing at any given time.

For instance, an inflationary cycle can easily erode the value of a long-term bond fund since interest rates on long-term bonds are locked in for years at a time. If the current interest rates rise (as they would in an inflationary period), the value of the bond fund declines. At that time it would be advantageous to be able to switch over to a good stock fund. But in cycles where the market is overvalued, stocks and stock funds can lose much of their equity, so a bond fund can help protect your assets. The ability to switch funds in these instances is essential.

If we hit an economic cycle in which the economy is severely depressed and we also have hyperinflation (due to our government printing money to pay its bills, as I believe it will), then the ability to shift a portion of your assets into high-growth funds may be the difference between saving your money or seeing it destroyed through inflation.

*I*f you're interested in reasonable growth and maximum security, I would recommend government-backed mutual funds.

For those in this asset range I recommend that you stay with the less aggressive (and less risky) funds. The most aggressive are often called *growth* or *speculative;* the less risky are commonly called *balanced.* A balanced fund means that it has a mix of many companies' stocks and has a portion of its assets in short-term bonds, as well as in stocks.

There are obviously many relatively secure investments that yield a good rate of return. Most of them require an acquired expertise that many people are not willing to achieve. For the majority of people, mutual funds simply represent a good investment that requires only a limited expertise—basically knowing which funds perform well.

Normally I recommend *no-load* mutual funds (those that have no up-front commissions) because these provide the least dilution of your initial investment capital. The reason no-load funds do not have a load (or up-front charge) is because they are not sold through commissioned sales people. They generally are sold only through direct sales with the parent company.

The disadvantage of no-load funds is that if you have a question there is no one who can assist you face to face. You must always talk to an agent by telephone. For many people this represents no problem. For others, and particularly some older people, they want to have a real live person explain the investment thoroughly, in which case the fee is justified. In general, any good fund held for seven years or longer will perform well, whether it is a load or no-load fund.

It would be very difficult in this book to advise you on any specific mutual fund companies since they often cycle up and cycle down. Instead, I will limit my specific recommendation to the sources that evaluate mutual funds: newsletters. For an average investor, one of the best resources is a monthly newsletter written by those who regularly track mutual fund companies' performances.

One of the best mutual fund newsletters I have found (at present) is "Sound Mind Investing." However, as you might surmise, I can attest only to its usefulness today and trust it will remain so in the future.

You will find a listing of several mutual fund newsletters in the Appendix. The type of investor to which they are aimed is noted. If you're going to do any investing in mutual funds, I heartily recommend that you subscribe to at least one of these publications and learn enough to make the majority of your own decisions. The small amount you will spend on a good newsletter can be your best investment over the long run.

GOVERNMENT SECURITIES

The question that retirees ask most is: Should I have all my money in secure investments? Usually the secure investments they are referring to are securities backed by the U.S. government, such as T-bills, CDs, or savings in an FDIC-insured bank.

I would certainly recommend that any funds you have in a ready asset account be in an insured institution. This would include money you need for emergencies or normal operating expenses. But to squirrel your major assets away in a fixed earnings account out of fear is poor stewardship. The certainty is that inflation will strip them of their value just as surely as a burglar can strip your home; neither announces their entrance.

Those who have large amounts of excess investment capital (more than they need to live on) can afford the luxury of very conservative investments; but those with marginal assets (or less) cannot afford the risk of inflation which, in my opinion, is the greatest risk any retiree faces in the next decade. In other words, Ross Perot can afford to park his money in T-bills because even if inflation erodes 75 percent of its value he still has several hundred million dollars left.

If you're interested in reasonable growth and maximum security, I would recommend government-backed mutual funds. These are funds that invest only in government securities, such as Ginnie Maes. See the Appendix for information on these funds.

TAX CERTIFICATES

In most counties throughout America, local governments offer tax certificates when property owners fail to pay their real estate taxes. These certificates are actually liens against the owners' property until the taxes are paid in full, with interest.

*P*erhaps no better investment can be made after retirement than developing an income-producing business.

Investors can bid on these tax certificates at auction and, after paying the taxes due, hold them as an investment. The interest rates are usually considerably higher than those available through other secured investments. The risk is that if the taxes aren't paid by the predetermined period (usually three to five years) you own the property. So you need to do a property evaluation before bidding on any certificates. Even so, in a severe economic downturn, such as we had in 1991, the fair market value of many properties actually dropped below the tax lien value, in which case the investors had to hold the properties for appreciation. If you need the income on a monthly basis, however, this would not be the best investment for you. Often the property owners will delay paying the certificates until the last possible date. This is particularly true with real estate developers who are short on cash in a downturn.

You can get more specific information on tax certificates in your area by calling your local county tax commissioner's office.

PERSONAL LOANS AND SECOND MORTGAGES

I have a friend in Atlanta who manages investments for several retired people, including several widows. Obviously he is very cautious with their money. Over the years he has developed a good steady source of income for them by investing in personal loans and second mortgages.

The principle is simple: He acts as a coordinator for the lenders and qualifies all the borrowers thoroughly, ensuring that each has a good credit history and adequate collateral. Then he actually drafts the loan agreements and collects the payments, for which he receives a small percentage.

This strategy is done on a small scale, and only the best risks are assumed. Still there are risks associated with this type of investing, as with any investment. To date he has not had a single borrower default, but that is always a possibility in the future.

In most areas of the country there are attorneys who handle transactions like this for lenders. The best way to find someone who does this is to ask in your church. Just be certain that this person has a long track record (at least ten years) and a virtually unblemished record. And limit this portion of your portfolio to no more than 15 percent of the total.

HOME BUSINESS

Perhaps no better investment can be made after retirement than developing an income-producing business. This does not mean lending money to your brother-in-law to start a

car wash. Find something that you can do and risk a small portion of your assets in yourself.

An example would be to invest in a direct sales business
such as Amway, Mary Kaye, Successful Living, or any other
proven company. Quite obviously this is not an area for everyone. You must have the ability and desire to sell to others and
be able to organize and train others—if you want the business
to expand. But for those who can do this, it will return their
investment thousands of times and has the ability to adjust to
inflation too.

There is no doubt that many of the direct sales plans have
been misused and been presented as "get-rich-quick" plans.
But the fact that one group abuses the concept does not mean
the idea is wrong. Just keep your priorities straight and these
businesses can be of great advantage to you as an investment.
Also use reasonable caution and don't go overboard by investing too much too soon. Start small and use your profits, not
retirement savings, to expand.

If getting into a direct sales company doesn't appeal to
you, look at other possibilities. For a small investment you can
go to a vocational technical school and study computer science
or television repair—or, learn how to be a plumber, electrician,
woodworker, painter, mechanic, or something you would enjoy
doing. Then, with a nominal investment in some tools or equipment, you may find an excellent part-time career in retirement.

Be sure you check out the licensing requirements in your
community before investing your time and money. But many
occupations such as painting, minor plumbing (faucet repairs),
or secretarial assistance usually have no special requirements.

RENTAL PROPERTIES

One of the most common questions I am asked is, "Is
rental property a good investment?" The obvious answer is "It
depends."

There are definite assets and liabilities in owning rental
property. The assets are diversification, appreciation, and allowing the rental income to pay off the properties. The liabil-

ities (especially for retirees) are high maintenance costs, area
deterioration and, most of all, the headaches of being a landlord.

*I*f you don't understand an
investment, pass it by, no matter
how good the deal sounds.

In past years rental properties did well for investors
through appreciation. But the high growth periods for real estate probably are gone for the foreseeable future. In fact we are
witnessing some significant devaluation in many areas. Rental
property can be profitable if it's totally debt-free, but the problems associated with maintaining rental units are many and,
unless you're a real "fix-it" type, I would recommend you avoid
investing in rental properties after retirement.

If you do decide to invest in a rental property, be sure it is
in a good location, qualify your renters just as you would a
potential buyer, and study the rules (laws) of renting in your
state.

OTHER INVESTMENTS

There are obviously other conservative investments that
can be used to bolster your retirement income. In virtually every case the risk is directly related to your knowledge about
that particular investment. It is very difficult for someone to talk
you into making a bad investment if you know what you're doing. So stay with what you know. If you don't understand an
investment, pass it by, no matter how good the deal sounds
and no matter how many other Christians are involved. The
most consistent error I have witnessed with those whom I have
counseled is investing because Christians were involved. Be-

lieve me, Christians can make as many bad decisions as anyone else and sometimes more.

$50,000 TO $100,000 IN INVESTMENT ASSETS

A word of caution is necessary if you fit into this group.
All too often those who have saved retirement funds through a
payroll deduction plan, and then receive it as a lump sum, look
at it as inexhaustible. Not only is it exhaustible, but it will evap-
orate so quickly it will startle you unless you're extremely careful and manage your funds carefully.

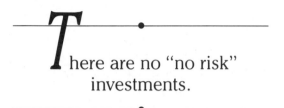

*T*here are no "no risk"
investments.

If you have never managed a large sum of money, my
advice is to park the funds in a good safe place for at least one
full year. Only invest your money after first investing your time
and effort to know what you're doing when you do invest.

As with the first group, the vast majority of the funds you
have will need to be invested for income unless your income
needs are satisfied totally through a pension plan and/or Social
Security, which is rarely the case.

In reality there is little difference in the investment strategy
of someone with $100,000 and someone with $50,000, except
that in the latter case less risk can be assumed. No one wants
to lose *any* money. But to lose 20 or 30 percent of your asset
base is one thing; to lose 50 to 75 percent is quite another.

With $100,000 to invest you should be able to generate
between $8,000 and $10,000 a year income without assuming
any unrealistic risks. If you attempt to earn more, it will almost
always require too much risk, so set realistic goals. Also bear
in mind that most people exaggerate when they mention their
own return on investments.

The one thing you should be able to achieve with more resources is greater diversification. If you will set a limit of say $10,000 per investment (maximum), the risk will then be spread into ten different areas. Even a loss of 50 percent in any one investment would only dilute your assets by 5 percent. The same requirement for flexibility exists as with a lower asset base. You simply won't have enough assets to park them in fixed earnings investments like CDs or T-bills and leave them there indefinitely. If you do, you'll find your income steadily declining in relation to the cost of living. Inflation, not depression, is your biggest enemy, and you need to protect against it diligently. In my opinion, that can be accomplished best through the use of good quality mutual funds.

Just as the three most critical factors in real estate investing are location, location, and location, the three most important factors in mutual fund investing are quality, quality, and quality! Don't risk your hard earned and virtually irreplaceable savings in new ventures. Stay with those who have at least a twenty-year proven track record of growth in good times and in bad.

The advantage you have with greater assets is greater diversification, even within mutual funds. You can diversify through several different companies and in such widely spread areas as utility companies, blue-chip companies, municipal bond funds, government funds, international funds, precious metal funds, and so on.

Since this chapter is discussing only investment strategy, rather than specific investments, I won't elaborate further. In the next chapter I'll try to share more about where to find the best investments to meet your goals.

One word of caution: There are no "no risk" investments —not even the FDIC is risk free. You must settle on how much risk you are willing to assume and then *stay flexible*! What works in one economic cycle can fail in the next. You can't just park your money and forget it. If you do, you probably *can* forget it because it will be gone!

$100,000 PLUS IN INVESTMENT ASSETS

The strategy for those with greater assets should shift somewhat. Retirees with lesser amounts to invest are forced by economic reality to take greater risks to stay even with inflation if they need to live off their earnings. But those with more funds to invest should develop a two-tier strategy.

The first tier is to secure the income you need. Let's assume for illustration purposes that you need $20,000 a year above what either a pension or Social Security will provide. (*Note*: this presumes that Social Security retirement benefits will still be available to this income group).

If the retiree in our illustration has $300,000 available, the first $200,000 or so should be invested primarily in secure, income-producing investments, such as utility company bonds, government bonds, or high quality corporate bonds. The same goals usually can be accomplished through high quality mutual funds that specialize in these investments, if you don't feel competent enough to make the selections yourself.

The additional $100,000 can be invested in areas that will have greater growth potential and can help to offset inflation, much like the earlier examples. The more surplus funds available, the more diversification and growth that can be achieved.

For those with amounts in excess of $500,000 to invest, I would suggest acquiring some international investments and precious metal funds that can help to offset the economic trends in the U.S. Again I would recommend good quality mutual funds for those who lack the experience and expertise to make these kinds of choices.

Retirees with assets in excess of several hundred thousand dollars almost certainly are going to see their Social Security benefits either reduced or at least the cost of living increases curtailed. Due to the voting power of older Americans, I would guess that the latter is more likely. It is extremely important, if and when this occurs, to keep your other assets in inflation-hedged investments. I know it seems that I am harping on this issue but I feel that I would be doing you a disservice if I didn't. You only need to read about the inflation cycle in other countries to realize how devastating it can be to those on retirement incomes, even with large surpluses. Too often retirees become paralyzed with the fear of losing their security, and they get even more conservative.

Obviously God is our resource, and He will provide for His people who are willing to trust Him. My function is to help you understand that we're a part of God's plan, not just observers of it. Use your mind to help avoid some of the pitfalls, if at all possible. If you have done all you reasonably can, God will still provide. But too often it's a Christian cop-out to declare, "We're just supposed to trust the Lord." Certainly we are, while doing all we can to help solve the problems. Remember the lesson taught in Proverbs 24:33-34, *"A little sleep, a little slumber, a little folding of the hands to rest, then your poverty will come as a robber, and your want like an armed man."*

An Inflationary Cycle

The following is a discussion with a businessman from Argentina. In the early 1980s Argentina suffered from a massive wave of hyperinflation. At one point prices on some items were rising 100 percent per *day*. Over an eight-year period Argentina saw an inflation rate of approximately 600,000 percent! There were intelligent, well-educated people living in Argentina—just as there are in our country now. Most of them never considered the effects of inflation on their lifestyles until it was too late. I pray we won't make the same mistakes. I have taken the liberty of paraphrasing the details of what he told me.

> My parents were average, working-class people who paid their taxes, went to church, and accepted government as an unapproachable aristocracy. They rarely went out to eat and only dreamed of owning their own home one day.
>
> When the government of Argentina first began to borrow money from the International Bank (The International Monetary Fund) in the early seventies, most Argentineans thought little about it. There were promises of prosperity and new roads, but there had been similar promises in the past, and all the average citizens saw were more taxes and a few roads leading to the politicians' land.

This time it was different. The amount of money Argentina was able to borrow started new projects: dams that employed thousands to build, roads across the countryside, public buildings that employed more Argentineans. But the greatest thing of all was that taxes didn't go up; instead they actually went down—unheard of in a South American country.

There seemed to be a newfound prosperity in Argentina. People who had never been able to save anything were suddenly able to find jobs paying twice what they had made before, working for the government. The government became the employer of preference for anyone seeking to get ahead.

The very politicians who were once looked upon as parasites became the heroes of the average working class. No one seemed to notice or care that Argentina was spending money it didn't have; prosperity abounded everywhere. The thought was, the rich nations of the world would not let us borrow unless they were sure we could pay it back. After all, they didn't get to be rich by being stupid, did they?

As the annual deficit figures continued to rise, some academic people began to say that Argentina was spending its way into poverty. But in general they were ignored as alarmists and terribly old fashioned.

When the debt to the World Bank reached $10 billion, the dooms-dayers predicted that the economy would go up in flames or something equally catastrophic; but that didn't happen either. Sure, the interest payments on the debt were large, but the government simply borrowed more money to cover the payments each year. Prosperity abounded and Argentina was "hooked on credit." The total debt soared past $10 billion and on into $20 billion, then $30 billion, then $40 billion. At each step along the way, the more conservative politicians and academicians shouted alarms, but the country was on a roll and the people were experiencing more prosperity than they had ever dreamed possible. Politicians who even thought about reducing the debt and spending were voted out and more progressive people were voted in.

In Argentina the thought of becoming another world economic power was being seriously discussed. Even my own normally conservative parents were borrowing heavily against the steadily increasing values of their new home and their small bakery business to speculate in land syndications. Taxes began to rise as some of the foreign credit dried up and most Argentineans complained; but prosperity was still the byword, so they paid the higher taxes and counted on economic growth to make up the difference.

The international loans, which had originally been meant to help Argentina develop its natural resources, instead went to government buildings, public assistance (welfare), and more bureaucrats to administer the programs. Roads were built primarily to create new jobs, not to develop new industry. The primary locations were those in the most influential politicians' districts.

Many of Argentina's citizens became direct beneficiaries of the new prosperity. In other words, they accepted government welfare not to work. My own parents sold their little business for a highly inflated price, and my father took a position with the government as an economic advisor.

Eventually, he retired with a comfortable pension and spent most of his time helping to put land deals together for friends and family. Everybody believed that the prosperity was unending; and it was, as long as the money held out.

Then, the plug was pulled. The World Bank was no longer willing to lend Argentina any more money. The debt to Central and South American countries substantially exceeded their total net worth, and there was no realistic way they would ever be able to repay their obligations.

Suddenly Argentina was unable to pay even the interest on its debt. But worst of all, the politicians could not continue the expansion that the Argentineans had grown to expect. Faced with the very real prospect of an internal rebellion, they took the only course that weak-willed officials could: They began to print the money they needed to pay the bills.

At first it seemed that once again the politicians had discovered the golden goose. The prosperity continued, and the borrowing stopped. But in many papers, warnings were sounded by those who had lived through the inflationary times in Germany and later in Brazil. But, with virtually no other choice, the printed money continued to flow.

The Argentine astral was devalued on the world exchange by more than 50 percent. The prices on virtually everything in the cities doubled overnight. Angry citizens demanded that the government do something, so price controls were instituted for food and fuel. The net result was that the supply of food and fuel (outside of the black market) dried up. No thinking merchant was going to sell his merchandise at discounted prices knowing that he would pay a premium to restock what he needed.

I can remember my father telling my mother not to worry. "Our future is secure," he promised her. "Our money is in land, and they don't make that anymore." But neither my parents nor anyone else could have foreseen the disaster that was about to overtake them: *hyperinflation.*

In the six months following the initial printing of money, Argentina's currency was devalued by more than 600 percent! Life for the average citizen became a struggle just to buy food and keep the utilities on. Four months later, keeping the utilities on became inconsequential as the cost of food escalated by some 6,000 percent. The entire life savings of most Argentineans was spent in less than six months, and then they had to sell every possession just to stay alive.

My own parents saw their fragile empire crumble as the cost of living soared beyond their ability to pay for even the basic necessities of life. Their land was repossessed, their home sold at auction to a banking cartel, along with several hundred others, and their government pension would not pay the tax on the food they needed. Life in Argentina became the worst nightmare the alarmists had predicted.

In 1989 the people of Argentina elected a dictator to reestablish control over the runaway economy. Only through stern price controls, backed up by stiff prison sentences, has the government been able to bring inflation under control. The currency has changed three times since the new government took over, and the middle class no longer exists.

Retirees in Argentina are no longer concerned about how to stop work. They are primarily concerned with how to find jobs that will allow them to live with some dignity. Most fear the growing trend in society toward disposing of the aged and the ill on the basis of economic necessity. Few retirees voice opposition to programs eliminating their benefits. They fear being eliminated themselves even more.

*R*isk is not necessarily bad, as long as you know what the probable risks are and can afford to assume them. The less you know about the investments you make, the harder it is to assess this risk.

CHAPTER ELEVEN
Where to Invest

I find it very difficult to discuss specific investments because even as I am writing the economy is changing. At present interest rates are down, inflation is down, land values are down, and the stock market is up. But that could change tomorrow and, to some degree, it certainly will by this time next year. Also our politicians may change the tax laws to enhance certain types of investments while devaluing others. I hope you can see why investment specifics are so difficult.

But, I personally don't like books that purport to be "how to" books but talk only in generalities, so I will try to avoid doing the same. Sometimes an author must talk in generalities because the potential audience for the material is too broad to be specific; and to some extent, this is true with a book on retirement. Some readers may only be thinking about retirement; others are already there. It is this last group that I would like address.

I will repeat (less I be misquoted later), that no one, NO ONE, has a good grasp on what will happen in our economy between now and the end of this decade. There are so many divergent ideas on how to fix our economy one can only guess at what changes, if any, will actually be made.

If the current trend in our government toward more spending and greater debt accumulation continues unabated, we will run out of money during the latter part of this decade. More than likely, I will revise this book about 1996 or so. By that time the deficits may well be running a trillion dollars or so a year, and interest on the debt will consume approximately 80 percent of all income taxes collected. Average Americans may be paying one-half of their incomes in direct taxes, and considerably more in hidden taxes on gasoline, utilities, and some form of value-added tax.

The investments that might normally work in a sane economy won't work in such an insane period as this, and if my analysis holds true, you'll need a survival-mode investment strategy. Until we really see whether or not fundamental changes will be made in our economy, the best I can do is help you to "hedge" and to stay as flexible as possible. This strategy is not possible without being specific.

Some investment advisors will disagree with my analysis of the economy and the specific advice I offer in this chapter. That's okay. Everyone has a right to disagree. The best I can do is tell you what I see and let you make up your own mind. The one thing I can say is that I personally have done many of the things I recommend and, thus far, they have worked for me, even with limited resources.

If you have more than $500,000 in investable assets you need more specific advice than I can give you in this type of book. I would suggest that you get a copy of *Investing for the Future* (Victor Books) and read it thoroughly. Then subscribe to several of the newsletters listed in the Appendix. In addition you need a good, professional investment advisor to help you make your decisions.

I believe that professional financial advice can be of great service to those with lesser assets. Unfortunately, they can seldom afford it, in which case written advice is an inexpensive substitute.

Before discussing some ways to generate income during retirement, I would like to lay out what I see as a typical portfolio for those who have limited assets but need good diversification.

Let's assume you're just about to retire and your company offers either an annuity for $1,300 a month for the rest of your life or a cash settlement of $150,000—the amount you have vested in the company benefit plan. Which should you take?

The specifics are as follows.

1. The annuity represents a 10.4 percent return on the amount you have in the account. This certainly is not a bad rate of return. In fact, you would have a difficult time finding an insurance company annuity that would match it.

2. You discover that the annuity initially offered is a single-life plan and would pay nothing to your widow if you predecease her. Taking a two-life annuity would drop the monthly payout to $1,100 a month—a yield of 8.8 percent, which is still okay but not great.

3. You also learn that the annuity payout is fixed—meaning that it cannot be changed once you accept it.

With all of the above facts in hand you decide to take the lump sum. Now that you have $150,000, what do you do with it?

INVESTMENT PLAN

Go to your bank and establish a *self-directed IRA*. You simply want a place to park the money until you decide where to invest it. You have 60 days to reinvest the funds in a tax deferred plan (IRA) or you'll have to pay the taxes and the early withdrawal penalty of 10 percent.

If your bank offers a self-directed IRA, you will need only to transfer the funds into one of their IRA money market accounts. Otherwise you would need to shop for a bank that has a self-directed IRA. All that is necessary to redirect the funds to the IRA is to fill out the transfer forms provided by the bank and they can be transferred that day.

We'll assume that some time passes, during which you do the appropriate study recommended in *Investing for the Future*. You probably have had several "hot tips" from friends and family, as well as loan requests from cash-poor relatives. I will assume you turned them all down and now you're ready to make some investments.

I believe that inflation is a higher risk to any retiree than virtually any other scenario (other than a loan to your brother-in-law).

After thorough investigation you decide to invest some of the retirement funds as follows:

a. $25,000 in a short term corporate bond fund paying 8 percent per year.
b. $25,000 in a high quality utility bond fund paying 8.6 percent per year.
c. $25,000 in "A" rated municipal bonds paying 6 percent per year (tax free).
d. $25,000 in a second mortgage repurchased from a local mortgage company paying 12 percent per year.
e. $25,000 in a growth mutual fund averaging 15 percent per year appreciation.
f. $25,000 will be kept in a U.S. government securities fund. The fund pays 7 percent per year and is totally accessible on a daily basis.

The net result of this strategy is an income of $8,900 a year in earnings from the taxable funds, another $1,500 from the tax-free fund, and approximately $3,750 in annual appreciation from the growth mutual fund. So you could realistically expect to have somewhere between $10,500 and $15,000 a year available to spend (depending on whether or not you sold some of the growth mutual fund shares to increase your earnings).

By varying the strategy we could either have earned more income (at a higher resultant risk) or taken virtually no risk by parking the money in CDs or T-bills.

As you already know, I believe that inflation is a higher risk to any retiree than virtually any other scenario (other than a loan to your brother-in-law); therefore, I would opt for a plan that will flex for inflation. In this case, any of the mutual funds could be shifted into more aggressive funds that can help to cope with some inflation.

The one great difficulty in any long-term financial plan is implementing it. I can show any number of ways to increase income or reduce expenses, but if you don't actually do something as a result, it's a waste of time. And it is an unfortunate fact of life that the majority of people implement very little of what they hear. To be fair though, I realize that most people want to do financial planning but they get paralyzed by all the options.

The plan just presented can be accomplished through any number of good quality mutual fund companies. A list of some of the best-rated companies is provided in the Appendix. I personally have invested with several of them over the years and have found their services to be excellent. I usually select only non-loaded mutual funds because I don't need the personal help that a local agent can provide.

But I have to be honest and say that some of the companies (mutual funds) I placed money in ten years ago are not performing as well as they once did. After carefully checking each of them I discovered that only one out of ten still matched its performance from five years earlier. I decided to find out why because, using a strategy known as *dollar-cost averaging,* I had been told that over a long period (seven to ten years) the funds would cycle down and then back up. By continuing to invest in both high and low periods (dollar-cost averaging), my return overall should stay constant.

The analogy is rather like flipping a coin. Sometimes you'll hit a succession of heads, sometimes you'll hit a succession of tails, but overall they will average out fifty-fifty—only mine didn't.

Recently a friend and I were discussing this very issue, and I found what he said very enlightening. It seems that any individual mutual fund company will do well with their strategy during one phase of the economy and poorly during another.

For example: One fund I invested in selected only quality companies that had an excellent price-to-earnings ratios. In other words, the stock prices were low compared to the companies' annual earnings. Therefore it was logical to expect the stock prices to increase, thereby generating a profit for their investors—in this case my mutual fund company. Since the fund manager traded companies based on their (stock) price-to-earnings ratio, he was able to generate gains and increase the value of the fund. If you need money from this type of mutual fund you have to sell some of your shares, which should be higher in value than what you paid.

What is needed is a fund so broad and diverse that you can take advantage of any market trend.

As I looked at the trend lines from the various funds, they were still appreciating, but most were down from their peaks of several years earlier. In other words, the funds were still profitable, they just weren't *as* profitable.

As my friend explained it, the problem is in the basic philosophy of the fund managers themselves. They had originally found a method that worked better than any other: in this case, price/earnings ratios, which were the rage with investors in the early eighties. Fund managers who used this selection process were very successful. But as time went by, the market shifted to other dynamics, such as high tech stocks. During the late eighties, investors didn't really care about price/earnings as much as they did the growth potential of companies. So the highest earners were in the high-tech companies.

By the early nineties the trend shifted to health-care-oriented companies and, although the high tech companies and companies with low price/earnings ratios stocks still appreciated, they didn't appreciate as much as before.

"How then," I asked my friend, "do you solve that basically unsolvable problem? The very thing that makes a good fund manager profitable in one phase eventually makes him unprofitable—or at least less profitable."

He responded, "There are two basic ways: One, you can fire the fund manager as soon as you see some other method working better than his; or two, you can seek out a mutual fund company so big and diverse that your investment is spread across the entire gamut of growth strategies, as well as different areas of the economy."

My response was that the first idea is rather hard on fund managers. I think it would be hard to develop much loyalty, knowing that they were going to be fired as soon as someone else did a little better in their investment philosophy.

He agreed and said studies also show that the cycles tend to repeat from time to time, so you just might need him again.

I agreed that the second idea was a good one, but for anyone smaller than IBM I assume that kind of diversification is almost impossible.

"Not really," he replied. "What is needed is a fund so broad and diverse that you can take advantage of any market trend. Certainly you won't maximize your return the way you might if all your money were in the yearly winner, but overall you'll do better and with less risk."

This concept piqued my interest since I'm a great believer in lowering risk wherever feasible—especially if you don't have to sacrifice too much return.

He shared how his financial firm had contracted with one of the largest money management companies in the world to place investor assets in their mutual funds. This company, the Frank Russell Company, then takes the money it manages and spreads it over many well-managed mutual funds (at present there are thirty-six) to take maximum advantage of the talents of the many mutual fund managers. The progression of lowering risk and increasing profits is shown in the diagrams below.

First, if you invest in one company you may make a profit. But if that company does poorly, you lose.

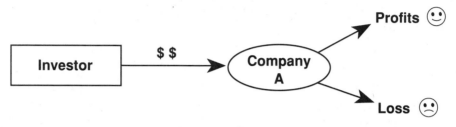

Then, you decide to invest in five companies to spread the risk.

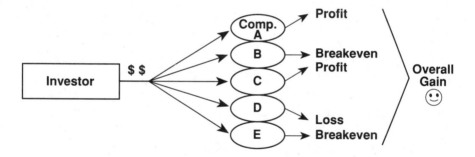

The potential profits may be smaller, but the risk is substantially lower, especially if you diversify by different industries too.

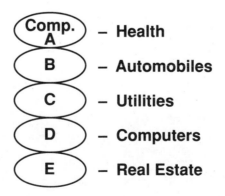

Since that is basically what a mutual fund company does for you, it is simpler to buy a mutual fund and let someone else manage the money.

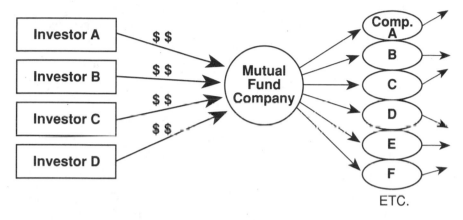

By pooling your money with a larger money manager, he then diversifies even more by allowing you to invest in many mutual fund companies.

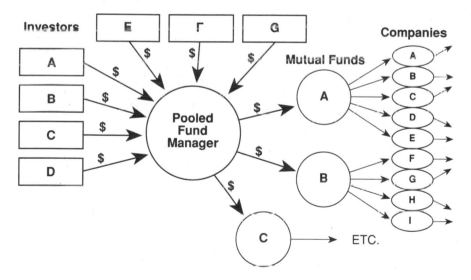

      Obviously both the money manager and the fund managers have to make money too. So if you pool your funds there will be a fee for the manager. So I asked, "How much does all this cost, and how much money does someone have to invest?"

It was interesting to find out that the total annual cost was no higher by pooling through the money manager than by using a good no-load mutual fund. The reason is that the money manager simply negotiated his fee along with the fund managers' fee, since he was able to provide large amounts of capital with virtually no cost to the fund managers.

The answer to the second question (about how much a single individual had to invest) was about what I would have thought: $50,000. This is because the money manager was pooling hundreds of individuals' funds together.

To my knowledge there is only one company now doing this pooling and then investing with one of the top three money managers in the country. There are probably others that I have not heard of yet. I have listed this firm in the Appendix (see Asset Management Services) for those who, like myself, are looking for maximum diversification with no additional costs. It would seem foolish not to investigate it.[1]

*F*ew retirees should seriously consider an insurance plan, other than an annuity, in which to invest their retirement funds.

I trust the trend in financial planning will continue to be toward the individual planner acting as a counselor and steering his or her clients toward the best possible investments with the least possible risk.

INSURANCE PRODUCTS

As I mentioned earlier, I try to avoid repeating information already available in other publications, but some overlap

---

1. The author does not attest to the profitability of the money manager or the fund companies. Investors must carefully evaluate this for themselves.

is unavoidable. There are a few investments that virtually every retiree will have questions about and insurance is one of them.

Separate from the death benefit side of life insurance is the investment benefit, or dividends of a cash value insurance policy. When an insurance company charges an amount in excess of the current premium, as they do in cash value insurance, that money can be invested and income earned on it. Since all insurance companies are competing for customers, they attract additional customers by returning a portion of what they earn (or expect to earn) in the form of dividends. In some of the newer policies issued since mutual fund companies came into existence, the returns are competitive with good quality mutual funds.

However, in my opinion, few retirees should seriously consider an insurance plan, other than an annuity, in which to invest their retirement funds. The cost of insurance consumes too much of their premiums. Basically there is not enough left over to invest and make a reasonable return. So the discussion here is not whether you should buy a cash value insurance policy as an investment after retirement; generally it is a poor investment. The question is: Should you keep a cash value policy already in force, or should you cancel it or at least draw out the cash portion and invest it elsewhere?

These decisions are really statistical ones. If the interest being earned within the insurance policy is equal to or greater than what can be earned in a relatively safe investment (CD, T-bill, or government securities), then there is really no profit in withdrawing it.

Generally, it has been my experience that if the insurance policy was issued before 1980 the earnings will be significantly below that of a good mutual fund. Obviously there are some individual exceptions, but insurance companies did not get competitive with their whole life plans until the mutual fund industry began to eat into their investment funds (around the early eighties).

Most insurance policies have a guaranteed return and an estimated return. With rare exception, the amount advertised is the estimated rate of return. More often than not, the figures an agent uses in promoting the policies are gross earnings, not net (the actual amount you are credited).

Gross earnings is the amount the company expects to earn before commissions and other fees are deducted.

Net earnings is what will actually accumulate to your account each year. This will be higher than the guaranteed amount but lower than gross earnings. Since these amounts can vary annually, you need to verify the actual figures in order to make your decision. Usually the insurance company will provide reports stating the net earnings figure each year. If you keep these reports they will provide the information you need.

The *guaranteed* rate is what the company must pay, irrespective of what their investments do. This is normally 3 to 5 percent per year, depending on the issue date of the policy.

If you have a question about the earnings on your life insurance policy, you should have your agent request a printout of these annual reports.

Your options in withdrawing the funds from a life insurance policy are twofold. You can cancel the policy, in which case the insurance company will surrender the net cash reserves and whatever earnings belong to you. (Of course this also cancels your life insurance.)

The second option is to borrow the cash reserves out of the policy. Usually the interest rate you will pay is about 2 percent more than the policy is paying you (may vary by company). In this case your insurance policy stays in force, but the death benefit will be reduced by the amount of the loan plus accumulated interest. Many people don't understand that they do not have to repay the loan or the interest. As long as the loan plus accumulated interest is less than the death benefit, the policy will remain in effect. Once the cumulative total exceeds the death benefit, the policy is canceled and the loans are canceled as well.

ANNUITIES

Since I have already covered the use of annuities as a source of retirement income, I will not elaborate again. Just remember: If you decide to use an annuity as a retirement investment, you need to verify the stability of the issuing insurance company at least once a year. The resources to do so are available in most public libraries (Rating Services listed in the Appendix).

If the insurance company is downgraded significantly, you may want to shift your annuity to another company. This is usually possible as long as the issuing company is still solvent. Any agent for the company of choice can usually do this for you.

In the event your insurance company fails, there is still a possibility of recovering some or all of your annuity. Check with your state insurance commissioner's office to see if your state has an insurance company pool fund to cover failed carriers. If not, you're probably limited to filing for recovery in the bankruptcy court.

RENTAL PROPERTIES

I will exclude from this discussion any mention of commercial real estate or undeveloped land. These investments normally are suitable for higher income investors, with a high degree of expertise in real estate. For the majority of retirees, there are simpler, less risky ways of generating the income needed.

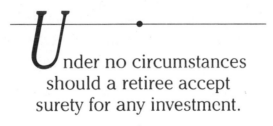

*U*nder no circumstances
should a retiree accept
surety for any investment.

As I said in the previous chapter, a debt-free single-family home or a multi-family dwelling, such as a duplex or triplex, is often a good source of retirement income for many people. There are obvious risks, the greatest of which is non-paying or destructive tenants but, in general, the risks are usually more mental than financial.

There is an old cliché in real estate that describes the three most important factors in buying rental property: location, location, location. This is fundamentally true. The ability to attract good tenants is primarily dictated by the location of your rental property; and good tenants are the key to any successful investment in rental property.

It is my opinion that the best use of rental properties is to buy them while you're still employed and use the rent from tenants to pay off the loans before retirement. However, since that isn't an option for current retirees, it is important to review whether or not rental properties are as good an investment as other options. There are basic rules to apply when making these decisions.

Allow no *surety*. Surety means taking on a contingent (future) liability. In other words, you have committed yourself to a debt without an absolutely certain way to repay it. In the case of rental property, the asset itself doesn't always cover the liability.

If you buy a rental home and finance it through a normal commercial lender, such as a bank, almost never will the lender accept the property as total collateral for the loan. This means that if for any reason you are unable to pay the loan as required, the lender has the right to recover the property, sell it, and sue you for any deficiency. That is surety according to Proverbs 22:26-27: *"Do not be among those who give pledges, among those who become sureties for debts. If you have nothing with which to pay, why should he take your bed from under you?"*

Under no circumstances should a retiree accept surety for any investment, whether it is a rental home or a gold mine in the Yukon. The last thing you want after working all those years is to have a creditor step in and seize your other assets when you can least afford it. The bottom line is: Don't take the risk.

Surety goes beyond just signing a note with a contingency agreement. For anyone in retirement it is critical to understand all contingencies. Often investments that seemingly have no contingencies can come back to haunt you—especially those involving the IRS.

A retiree I'll call Willard came to see me in the late eighties with a sad tale about surety and contingent liabilities. It seems that Willard had bought several limited partnership shares in various rental properties from a Christian investment advisor in his church. At the time, the properties looked like good investments since real estate, and particularly rental properties, were selling well and the income from the properties, along with the tax deductions, yielded nearly 20 percent return per year. Also the fact that the investments were in limited partnerships appealed to Willard because his financial liability was limited only to the money he invested. In other words, he had no financial responsibility to the partnership beyond his initial investment. However, the properties themselves had large outstanding mortgages on them which, in Willard's case, created a contingent liability of its own.

For nearly four years the properties did very well—not only paying the existing loans but returning some net income to the partners. Then in 1986 the Tax Reform Act changed the laws regarding passive loss write-offs against earned income, and partnerships in real estate took a tumble. Investors with sizeable incomes, such as doctors, pilots, business people, and others could no longer use passive losses, such as depreciation, to reduce their tax liabilities on earned income, as the previous tax laws allowed.

As new rental properties came on the market, many were repossessed by lenders since thousands of limited partnerships failed. The lenders, desperate to fill empty properties, slashed rents. Unfortunately many older properties like those Willard had an interest in became increasingly difficult to rent. Within a few months, several of the partnerships Willard was involved with failed.

Willard lost his investment in these properties which, in itself, was a severe financial setback, but over the next few months he also learned a costly lesson in tax law. Not only did the IRS come after the partners for recapture of much of the depreciation they had claimed on the rentals, but they also assessed them for "phantom income." According to the tax codes, when a debt is forgiven (in this case the loans on the properties), income is generated to the owners, including the limited partners.

Willard's tax bill for his share of the partnership's recapture came to nearly $40,000—a tremendous sum for someone living on $25,000 a year. He was able to pay the taxes only by selling off other assets. His income took a substantial cut. Not only did he lose the income from the partnerships, he lost the income from the additional $40,000 that went to taxes as well.

The moral to this story is simple: Know what the contingent liabilities are—all of them!

The obvious question any potential real estate investor must ask at this point is: Can you ever buy real estate without a contingent liability on the loan? Usually the answer is: only if the property is financed by a private individual.

The only way to avoid the contingent liability to the IRS is to ensure that you don't allow mortgaged property to go back to the lender unless you have the resources to pay the taxes if necessary. In other words, any mortgaged rental properties should be a very small portion of your retirement portfolio.

Since bad tenants can turn a good investment sour quickly, you should always qualify your renters, just as if they were borrowing money from you. Do a credit check on them once they have met any other criteria you set (children, pets). You can purchase credit information from agencies such as TRW and Equifax (listed in the Appendix) for a modest sum. The $50 or so you will invest in a credit check may well save you several hundred dollars in uncollected rents. You should also require references from other landlords, and it is well worth the cost of a phone call to check at least two of them.

Note: Often people are reluctant to provide negative information on former tenants because they fear retaliation (or even a potential lawsuit) if they do. But if you ask, "Would you be willing to accept them as tenants again?" most people will give you a straight yes or no. A no is usually the sign not to accept them as tenants yourself.

One last note about rental properties: If you don't have the temperament to evict a non-paying tenant, then you probably should not invest in rental units. Eventually you will have to evict a non-paying tenant. That, plus the work and time associated with maintaining a rental, is why I will never become a landlord, if I can help it.

The best strategy for rental properties I ever heard is that used by a friend in Atlanta. He prices his homes well below the current rental market so he can be very selective of his tenants. His tenant turnover rate is nearly zero and he has maintained some renters for more than ten years. This arrangement is truly a win-win situation for both sides.

GOVERNMENT SECURITIES

As I mentioned earlier, many retirees need absolute security in their investments since the money they have cannot be replaced and they don't have the temperament to take risks. Usually government securities represent the best overall investment for them.

There are four basic government notes of credit sold to the public: Treasury bills (T-bills), Treasury bonds (T-bonds), and savings bonds. The first two can be purchased through any regional Federal Reserve bank. Savings bonds can be purchased through virtually any bank.

T-bills are generally short term loans made to the U.S. government. The minimum purchase is $10,000, with multiples of $5,000 thereafter. The maturity on these notes is ninety days, one hundred eighty days, or one year, and the average interest rate is usually slightly less than that of the same size and duration CD.

T-bonds are usually issued in $1,000 units or more and have a maturity of seven to twenty-five years. The interest rates are higher due to the longer maturation period.

EE savings bonds are issued in denominations of $25 or more, with maturation periods of seven years or more. Unlike the T-notes and T-bonds, savings bonds and T-bills accumulate the interest and pay the face amount (principle and interest) upon redemption. It is of interest to note that the method by which savings bonds accumulate interest is not uniform, and if you cash them in between distribution periods (normally every six months), you will lose the undistributed interest. In other words, if you cash them in one day before the interest is distributed, you may forfeit six months of earnings.

There is a company, The Savings Bond Informer, that will evaluate U.S. savings bonds for you and advise on when to cash them in (see the Appendix for more information).

There are other government-backed investments available through most national stock and bond brokerage firms. These are government-backed loans issued by agencies such as the Government National Mortgage Association (GNMA)— hence the name Ginnie Mae. Ginnie Maes can be purchased in amounts of $25,000 or more with average maturity dates of about twelve years.

*I*n my opinion most retirees would be better served by investing in a mutual fund that invests primarily in government securities, rather than buying the securities directly.

There are also bonds issued by other government mortgage groups that can be purchased through brokers. These include the Student Loan Marketing Association (Sallie Maes), and the Federal National Mortgage Association (Fannie Maes). These bonds normally pay a higher rate of interest than T-bills and T-bonds.

Fannie Maes are not backed by the federal government, but it seems highly improbable that the government would permit a default on Fannie Mae obligations.

The negative side of government-issued loans is that the borrowers have the right to prepay their loans at any time. So a high interest note may be retired by refinancing it during a low interest period. You would then receive your principal back to reinvest.

GOVERNMENT-BACKED MUTUAL FUNDS

In my opinion most retirees would be better served by investing in a mutual fund that invests primarily in government securities, rather than buying the securities directly. This provides much more flexibility and since the mutual fund manages thousands of bonds and notes, it tends to level out the fluctuations during economic cycles. Be certain when you invest in a government-backed mutual fund that the fund actually owns the investments (as opposed to repurchasing them from a bank or other holder). Just ask the broker to ensure that the fund is a primary owner of the government notes.

Let me clarify something. I am not an advocate of lending the government any more money. If I had my way, I would try to convince all Americans to cut off the government's credit to force them to live on what they can raise in taxes and fees. However, since one purpose of this book is to explore the alternatives available to retirees, I have tried to cover the topic of government-backed investments in a reasonably unbiased fashion. Investors need to decide for themselves how they feel about our government heaping more debt upon our children and grandchildren. Personally I think it is the height of selfishness. We spend the money now; they pay later.

WHERE TO STORE READY CASH?

One of the most common questions asked is: Where should I put the money I need for emergencies or normal living expenses?

The options are limited since the money has to be available quickly: a checking account at a local bank, a savings account at the bank, a money market account at a bank, or a money market mutual fund at a stock brokerage firm. Or, if you belong to a credit union, that's another available option.

Exactly where to store the money is difficult to determine precisely. But there are some rules to follow:

1. Always keep any sizeable amount of funds ($5,000 or more) in an insured account (FDIC or equivalent).

2. Seek the highest rate of return with no greater degree of risk. This will normally be a money market account, as opposed to a savings account with your local bank. If you don't mind the fact that most of the money market mutual funds with large brokerage firms are not insured, these often pay a slightly higher rate of interest. Personally I consider them as safe as the FDIC.

3. Diversify if you have more than $25,000 to store in any account. I realize the FDIC insures accounts up to $100,000, but the more diversified you are, the safer your assets are going to be. Plus, if you have $100,000, it should be invested more wisely than it would be in a money market mutual fund.

RISK AND RETURN

Before concluding this brief description of possible investments for retirees, I want to comment on the most important principle of investing: The more return you seek on your money, the greater the risk you will assume.

I believe some risk is both necessary and prudent (especially in light of future inflationary periods), but the rules never change about risk and return. Anytime you seek to increase your rate of return you must, by virtue of our free market system, assume some more risk.

Risk is not necessarily bad, as long as you know what the probable risks are and can afford to assume them. The less you know about the investments you make, the harder it is to assess this risk. Conversely, the more you know, the easier it is. As Proverbs 24:3-4 says, *"By wisdom a house is built, and by understanding it is established; and by knowledge the rooms are filled with all precious and pleasant riches."*

There are many excellent resources available in the way of books, magazines, and newsletters, all of which can be purchased for less than $100. When you're considering investing thousands or tens of thousands of irreplaceable dollars, it is worth the time and cost to do some studying. Some of those I use are listed in the Appendix. I encourage you to check them out for yourself.

*T*he Lord can give you wisdom in this area of additional income. Take the time to pray and ask for His guidance. *"Trust in the Lord with all your heart, and do not lean on your own understanding. In all your ways acknowledge Him, and he will make your paths straight"* (Proverbs 3:5-6).

CHAPTER TWELVE

Untapped Income Sources

Mary Worth was a widow living on a small pension from a department store chain where she had worked most of her life. She also qualified for minimum Social Security benefits, which automatically qualified her for Medicare. Even so, Mary essentially lived in poverty, as many elderly do today.

Just the ordinary deductible amounts required by Medicare created financial burdens for Mary; she rarely had ten dollars extra to spare in any given month.

I met Mary after her pastor called and asked if I would be willing to meet with her to discuss her financial needs. He knew she probably was doing without some basic necessities, but she rarely mentioned her personal problems. Actually it was one of the other women in Mary's Methodist Women's group who approached the pastor. She had visited Mary while she was recovering from minor surgery and discovered that Mary had little or nothing left to buy food with after paying on her doctor bills.

Since the church had no permanent benevolence funds, the pastor had offered to help her out of his own funds, but she refused his offer. The pastor shared that when he offered to help, Mary said, "You need your money, Pastor. The Bible says that a workman is worthy of his hire." She insisted that she was doing fine and that her needs were being met.

The pastor asked her to at least see a Christian financial counselor. It just happened that she listened to our daily radio broadcasts, so when he suggested that I might be able to help she agreed.

Mary was a thoroughly delightful person. At 73 she was as alert and active as anyone I had ever met. She had a warm spirit and a love for the Lord that permeated everything she did. She was involved with a group that regularly visited several local nursing homes, and she had consistently attended a women's Bible study for nearly thirty years, often taking other women who needed the fellowship.

I asked her, "Mary, how much income do you have monthly?"

"I have enough to get by," she replied.

Having been through this procedure many times, I responded, "If I'm going to help you I need to know exactly what your financial situation is. How do you know that the Lord didn't send me to see you for just such a time as this?"

*I*t was clear that Mary had some financial problems she was not going to be able to handle by herself.

Mary immediately recognized the passage I had paraphrased from the book of Esther where Mordecai asked his cousin, *"And who knows whether you have not attained royalty for such a time as this?"* (Esther 4:14). She said, "Maybe you're right. I have been praying that God would help me pay my bills."

She told me that she had a total income of $412 a month, out of which she tithed, paid her utilities, bought her food, paid her property taxes and insurance, and made payments on her medical bills. The sum left over each month was zero.

In talking with Mary later, I learned that she owed nearly $3,000 in medical bills, on which she paid $20 a month. To most families, that $20 represents little more than a couple of trips to McDonald's. To Mary it represented a major portion of her food money.

Mary had stopped driving her car because she could no longer afford to repair it or pay the insurance on it. When she had a doctor's appointment, she took a cab to the bus station and rode the bus from there. When she visited the nursing homes, she rode with one of the other women; but she was always careful to give them some money for gas.

Mary had no close family; she was the youngest of six sisters, all of whom had died. The only assets that had sustained her in previous years were from a very small inheritance left her by one of her sisters and the home she had inherited from another sister. Mary's husband had died after they had been married only three years (nearly fifty years earlier), and she had never remarried.

It was clear that Mary had some financial problems she was not going to be able to handle by herself. I calculated that if she sold her home, she would probably net $80,000 after all the fees were paid. Invested securely, that amount of money could earn $7,000 to $9,000 a year. For Mary, that would be a fortune. After paying rent of perhaps $4,000, she would still have approximately $300 a month to live on. Even if she used $3,000 of the money to pay off her medical bills, she would still have enough left to net $250 a month or more. Since I had done this analysis between counseling sessions, I was excited to share my idea with Mary. When she came in the next week, I explained my plan. But then we hit a snag: Mary didn't want to sell her home.

One of the last wishes of her sister (who left her the home they had been living in together) was that Mary would keep the home as long as she lived. She had told Mary many times that she should *not* sell her home. She loved Mary and was fearful that someone might trick her out of her property. To Mary a promise was a promise—period. The issue of selling the home was settled. She had given her word.

I met with Mary several more times over the next few weeks, and by that time the women of her church had taken up some money to help meet her basic needs. Since Mary would not accept their money, they used it to buy groceries and other necessities for her. They even went to the drugstore where she had her prescriptions filled and set up an account in her name, which they paid.

This resolved the immediate problem of her basic needs, but it didn't solve the long-term problem of transportation, home repairs, and perhaps a periodic trip or vacation some-place. Mary never even considered traveling since she had so few resources. But she confessed one day that, if she had been able, she would have traveled with some of the other women from time to time.

Without exception, when I teach or counsel, I claim a promise that the Lord made in James 1:5, *"But if any of you lack wisdom, let him ask of God, who gives to all men gener-ously and without reproach, and it will be given to him."* So I started asking God to give me wisdom about how to help this dear lady. He did so one day while I was reading the *Wall Street Journal,* of all things. The answer He gave is one that can be of potential benefit to many retirees.

REVERSE MORTGAGES

The *Wall Street Journal* article discussed the concept of an older person selling his or her home through what was termed a *reverse mortgage.* The way a reverse mortgage works is the buyer commits to paying a monthly annuity to the seller (homeowner), based on the homeowner's age. When the homeowner dies, the house belongs to the buyer. Any residual value above the annuity payout already received becomes a part of the decedent's estate.

For example, if the home is appraised at $100,000, the reverse mortgage lender might pay $75,000 for the home (based on life expectancy). If the homeowner lives longer than expected and collects more than the projected $75,000, the lender loses.

If the homeowner dies sooner than projected, the difference between the actual amount paid and the actuarial value of the home ($75,000) is paid to the estate after the home is sold. So if the homeowner received $50,000, the lender would owe the estate $25,000 after the sale of the home.

In Mary's case, her home appraised for $105,000 and the reverse mortgage lender was willing to pay $68,000, based on her life expectancy. This translated into a $500-a-month annuity for life. As I explained to Mary, it was a win-win situation. She retained a life estate (the right of occupancy for life) and also got paid a monthly income. This arrangement satisfied her sister's request and her own need. She agreed to do it.

The real benefit of a reverse mortgage is that the seller retains the right to live in the home for life while living on the accumulated equity.

A reverse mortgage is not for everyone. In Mary's case, she had no immediate heirs to whom she wanted to leave her home, and she was not threatened by the fact that someone was buying her home while she lived there.

The income (in Mary's case) was not taxable since it was actually a loan against the value of her property.

In 1990 the Housing and Urban Development Commission (HUD) initiated a loan guarantee program designed to encourage more lenders to make reverse mortgages available. The loans are guaranteed by the Federal Housing Authority (FHA) and therefore make reverse mortgage loans much more accessible.

The AARP has a brochure available which explains the details of home reverse mortgages. Just write to: Home Made Money, AARP Equity Conversion Service, 601 E St NW, Washington DC 20049.

THE SHARED ANNUITY CONCEPT

A woman I'll call Naomi was a 73-year-old widow who had recently lost her husband. Because his pension stopped after he died, her total income was reduced by nearly 40 percent. She was left with only one real asset: her home, worth approximately $200,000, for which they had paid $28,000 in 1959.

She could have sold her home but she had no desire to move at such a late stage in her life, and there were no lenders offering reverse mortgages in her area of the country. Her home was located not far from a major university that sent out information periodically on their shared annuity program, which they promoted to nearby residents.

Naomi saw one of the school's brochures and asked my opinion about it. I told her it looked like a good idea and then made contact with the university's financial services office on her behalf. The arrangement that was ultimately made turned out to be a great deal for Naomi and the university.

Naomi entered into a contractual agreement with the school for a life annuity in exchange for donating her home to the university. The terms of her agreement allowed her to live in the home for the rest of her life, and she also received an annuity of $8,000 a year for life. In addition she also received a sizeable tax deduction for the remainder value of her home. This is the residual value of the home the school receives, based on her life expectancy.

During the eighties a unique business developed to help terminally ill patients generate income from their life insurance while they are still living.

Although Naomi was still responsible for maintaining the home and paying the real estate taxes, she netted nearly $5,000 a year in spendable income. The home will become the property of the university when she dies.

Obviously this is not a plan for everyone either. Naomi had no close heirs to whom she would have left her home, so that was not a consideration. Unfortunately she was not in a tax bracket (basically zero) where the deductions would help her financially. But, for higher income people, the tax incentives also can be of great value.

LIFE INSURANCE BUYOUTS

During the eighties a unique business developed to help terminally ill patients generate income from their life insurance while they are still living. This concept, called *living benefits*, has been an effective way for many terminally ill people to live out their lives in relative comfort: They sell their life insurance proceeds while they're living.

Recently some insurance companies (about 100 nationwide, as of this writing) also offer a similar benefit to their policyholders who are not terminally ill. The concept is simple: the company will buy out the policy by offering an annuity instead of a death benefit. So instead of having a life insurance policy, you convert to a life annuity. Obviously the company is doing this to lower their costs, but if you don't have a need for the life insurance, this can be a good source of additional income.

As of this date, the monthly proceeds from such an annuity are considered to be earned income and, as such, subject to income taxes. Depending on other earned income, this could also affect your Social Security income.

In the event the insured dies prior to the total annuity value being paid out, the remainder will go to the designated beneficiaries.

A call to your insurance company's customer relations representative will determine if your company offers this option presently. I rather suspect that as more companies provide this option, others will adopt it also. Just be certain that your need for life insurance has been satisfied before converting your policy.

CHARITABLE TRUSTS

Generally speaking, the type of trusts I will address here are most beneficial to those who have significant retirement income, since some of the benefits are tax deductions. However, if you need more current income and have already made the decision to give a portion of your estate to your church or other charitable organization, these trusts can be of great benefit to you and the ministry.

There are a myriad of charitable trusts available from virtually every major charitable organization in the country. In most cases, if you're serious about establishing a trust with a specific organization, they will provide all of the legal advice to do so. Some will even have the legal documents drafted at no cost to the donor.

If you are interested in more specific details than you find here, write the organization and request information. I have listed in the Appendix a few of the larger Christian organizations that offer these services. When you write, ask for their brochures on "charitable trusts."

CHARITABLE REMAINDER UNITRUST

This is one of the most common types of charitable trusts available today, and it is also the most flexible. Virtually any asset of value can be placed in a charitable remainder unitrust, with several options for receiving a lifetime income. I would like to use a practical example.

Bob was a 68 year old widower and a long-time supporter of a major evangelistic ministry. He owned a tract of commercial property he had purchased nearly thirty years earlier at a fraction of its current value. Bob had been approached by several developers about buying the property, but he had held out, thinking that one day it would be a prime prospect for a small shopping center.

Although Bob had an adequate retirement income, he had a need for a small amount more and also a desire to see his primary asset used to benefit the Lord's work after his death. After reading a letter from the planned giving department of the evangelistic organization, he contacted them asking for their counsel. The next time one of their field representatives was in the area he contacted Bob. After briefing him on the benefits of a charitable trust, Bob indicated that he was interested, if the details could be worked out. The first step was to arrange for the property to be appraised.

The appraisal came back at nearly $500,000—a surprise to even Bob. The ultimate arrangement worked to the benefit of the ministry, Bob, and the Lord's work.

If Bob had sold the property for $500,000, the taxable proceeds would have been $475,000 in capital gains (the sales price less the $25,000 he paid for the property). Obviously that would have placed him in the maximum tax bracket. His total tax rate would have jumped to approximately 40 percent (federal and state). So he would have paid nearly $190,000 in income taxes.

Instead, by donating the property to the charitable organization, he received a charitable tax deduction of approximately $260,000 (the remainder value of the property at his death) and a lifetime annuity of $2,500 a month. The tax deduction then could be used to offset much of his regular income, plus the annuity income for up to seven years. In addition, he avoided any capital gains tax on the transaction.

The amounts of the immediate deduction, as well as the monthly annuity, are variable—depending on the value of the assets assigned to a trust, the age of the donor, and whether it is a one- or two-life annuity. More recent transactions such as this may also be subject to the alternative minimum tax rules imposed by the 1986 Tax Reform Act. For specific details you will need to contact either the charitable organization or a qualified estate planning advisor.

In the case of a charitable remainder unitrust, the annuity is dependent on the amount of money actually available in the trust. Unlike an annuity where the income is guaranteed for the life of the annuitant, irrespective of the income from the asset, this type of trust limits the liability of the charity to the funds available. Obviously this is a negative for the donor but I personally believe it is an asset since, as Christians, we would not want a ministry to be saddled with an obligation beyond the funds committed to them. However, you must also be certain that the organization you choose to handle your trust is capable and well managed. Generally this will limit you to using larger organizations. If you desire, you also can name more than one organization as beneficiary in a charitable trust.

CHARITABLE GIFT ANNUITIES

Just as you can purchase an annuity through an insurance company, you can also purchase an annuity through many charitable organizations. The advantage is that a large portion of the profit accrued through the annuity then goes to the charity.

Usually the charity will actually purchase an annuity through an insurance company themselves, thereby limiting their contingent liability for future payments. If you decide to use a charitable gift annuity, just be certain that the insurance company underwriting the contract is a quality company.

UNPROFITABLE PROJECTS

Since many older Americans are in need of extra income, they become prime targets for scam artists selling everything from government surplus food to condominiums in Florida. Most of these scams follow very similar patterns.

The basic premise is that a company wants to use you as a test customer. This usually involves the sale of home repairs, equipment, or even encyclopedias. The salespeople call to make contact and offer to have their company put siding on your house, replace your roof, or place a set of encyclopedias in your home to use for demonstration purposes.

The salespeople assure you that this will cost you absolutely nothing. In fact, they say you will be able to generate income simply by making your home available as required. The promised rewards are often in the hundreds of dollars a month. Sound too good to be true? Well, that's because it is.

The hook in this bait is that you have to sign a good faith contract insuring the value of the product if any unreasonable damage occurs. More often than not there is also some substantial deposit required at the very last minute.

Almost before the salesperson is out the door, the contract is sold to a third party—usually a shell company owned by the first group. Then the billing starts thirty days later, along with some legal-sounding warnings about what can happen if the payments are not made. So, instead of this being an income-generating product, it becomes a cash drain for unnecessary work done. If this has already happened to you, contact your state consumer affairs department, as well as the state attorney general's office, and file a formal complaint. You also need to hire an attorney to represent you and go to court to cancel the contract.

*S*ince many older Americans are in need of extra income, they become prime targets for scam artists.

There are many other scams aimed at retired people, including the sale of government assets, drug confiscation sales, and so on. The common thread that runs through virtually all of these is the necessity to pay something up front for the service or information. I have investigated dozens of these get-rich-quick schemes and, to date, I have found none that are worthwhile (to put it mildly).

Unless you decide to get into direct marketing sales through reputable companies such as Amway, Mary Kaye Cosmetics, Shaklee, Successful Living, or several others that have been around long enough to prove their validity, very likely you will end up losing some of your money—and some of your friends as well.

I have a retired friend, James Acton, who came up with a relatively simply way to supplement his retirement income. James has always been interested in cars and, periodically, has sold one or two used cars when the opportunity has presented itself. He knows that when people have cars to sell they usually don't know exactly how to go about it.

Since knowledge and need make for opportunity, James began a small business by taking cars on consignment and selling them. After he had sold a few cars for friends, he decided to advertise his service through his church's bulletin board. Several people responded to the notice, and James settled on three good cars with which to start his home enterprise. He simply parked the cars on the vacant lot next to his home with "For Sale" signs in the windows. He then interfaced with the perspective buyers.

When a buyer was serious about a car, James put him in direct contact with the owner, who then completed the transaction. For James's part, he received a $150 commission. For the last several years he has sold between two and three cars a month for other people, with an average investment of not more than two hours per car. Since his reputation has grown, James now has both buyers and sellers calling him regularly. Because he's very selective about the cars (and people) he will interface for, people know they can trust what he says. James is not a used car salesman. He merely puts willing buyers and sellers together.

James took some of his spare time and turned it into a very profitable venture, without paying anyone franchise fees or up-front costs. He did have to secure the proper permits and a city license, but the total annual cost for his business is less than $100.

The Lord can give you wisdom in this area of additional income. Take the time to pray and ask for *His* guidance. *"Trust in the Lord with all your heart, and do not lean on your own understanding. In all your ways acknowledge Him, and he will make your paths straight"* (Proverbs 3:5-6).

*F*or those already on Social Security retirement, I believe we will sacrifice to maintain their incomes. But for those facing retirement beyond this decade, it is difficult to envision where the funds will come from.

CHAPTER THIRTEEN

Social Security Benefits

There never has been a social welfare program on the scale of the Social Security system. Retirement, Medicare, and disability payments now consume in excess of 40 percent of the total U.S. government's spending. Some people may take offense at my use of the term "social welfare," but that's exactly what Social Security is (as declared by the Supreme Court).

Until 1986 the Social Security system was funded on a pay-as-you-go basis—meaning that current contributions were sufficient only to cover current expenditures. In the mid-eighties the special committee appointed by President Reagan determined that when the "baby boomers" born after World War II began to reach retirement age, the system would not be capable of pay-as-you-go funding. The reason was determined to be twofold. First, there would be a huge influx of retirees—all from approximately the same time period. Second, there would be a steady decline in the number of active workers to replace them.

More recent figures from the Social Security Board of

Trustees show the problem to be far more acute than was accessed by the previous panel.

The 1991 Social Security Board of Trustees' Report reflects several converging factors that will drastically affect the system. I will attempt to summarize some of the more pertinent ones. If you require more verification I would encourage you to secure a copy of this report. Contact your regional Social Security office or write to: The Social Security Administration, 300 North Greene St., Baltimore, MD 21201 and ask for a copy of the 1991 Social Security Board of Trustee's Report on Social Security and Medicare.

*T*here are many more
potential retirees in the first
decade of the next century than
the present system can handle.

You may also want to request a copy of the Board of Trustee's Report on Social Security Trust Funds. However, the truth is: There aren't any. Each year the government takes the surpluses, spends them in the general revenue budget, and then substitutes worthless (in my opinion) IOUs for the actual funds. I question that a government that already has issued over $4 trillion in IOUs can ever repay the Social Security Trust.

For those already on Social Security retirement, I believe we will sacrifice to maintain their incomes. But for those facing retirement beyond this decade, it is difficult to envision where the funds will come from. We are facing what appears to be some unsolvable contingencies.

CONTINGENCIES

1. There are many more potential retirees in the first decade of the next century than the present system can handle. When the Social Security system began, there were approxi-

mately fourteen workers for every retiree (over the succeeding ten years). As of 1992, there are approximately four workers per retiree, and in the year 2000 it is estimated there may be only two active workers per retiree.

2. Even with a ratio of only two workers per retiree in the next decade, there is an additional problem. The American population is shifting more than at any time in the last century. Due to abortion and birth control, fewer children are being born per family unit in the U.S., and the gap is being filled by immigrants—a population base that contributes less to the tax system than native-born Americans do. (Generally it requires one entire generation before immigrants are fully assimilated into our population and can hope to achieve the same income levels.)

3. The entire economy of the U.S. seems to be shifting toward more service-related jobs, as compared to manufacturing jobs. This tends to create more jobs but at lower overall wages. Thus the income per active worker is actually less in terms of real contribution. As the graph below indicates, real income is steadily declining.

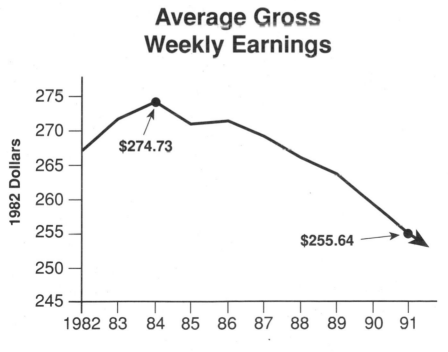

Average Gross Weekly Earnings

Source: Dept. of Labor, Bureau of Labor Statistics

4. The cost of health care is exceeding the average annual inflation rate by 200 to 300 percent. This cost, when factored into the Medicare system, will result in either much higher contributions on the part of wage earners (estimated to be between 26 and 32 percent according to the Board of Trustee's report), or higher costs to the Medicare recipients (dollar amount not available).

The cost of AIDS to the Medicare system is almost impossible to calculate. The average cost of caring for symptomatic AIDS patients is estimated to be somewhere between $125,000 and $250,000 (depending on the source of information) during a two-year period. The CDC estimates there are one to one and one-half million Americans now infected with the HIV virus. Most of them are expected to develop symptoms by the year 2000, assuming that no cure is found.

As I said previously, the Social Security Trust funds considered necessary for those who will be retiring beyond the year 2000 have been "borrowed" by the U.S. government. In their place, U.S. Treasury bills have been substituted. There is

The Cost of Medicare

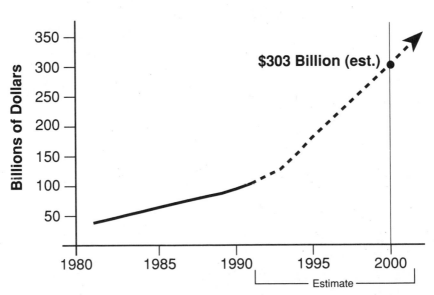

Sources: Dept. of the Treasury, Office of Management and Budget, Health Care Financing Administration

realistically little hope that these funds can ever be repaid since, in fact, they are part of the systematic overspending by our government. I personally believe it is naive to think that somehow our government will stop its foolish spending just before the need for these funds arrives.

I can see no real alternatives that would allow the baby boomers to enter the system. Social Security simply cannot absorb the costs of these retirees.

I could go on enumerating the various problems facing the Social Security system in the next decade and on into the next century, but I hope you see the picture the way it really is. If you have any doubts about the accuracy of my comments, please secure a copy of the reports yourself. If you can draw any different conclusions I would be happy to hear from you. I would also recommend that you get a copy of *Social Insecurity*, by Dorcas Hardy. As past commissioner of the Social Security Administration, certainly Mrs. Hardy should know if the system is solvent or not.

WILL SOCIAL SECURITY FAIL?

It is my considered opinion that the Social Security system itself will not fail for those who are recipients prior to the turn of the century. It will be supported at all costs by politicians anxious to avoid the voting wrath of the current retirees.

However, I can see no real alternatives that would allow the baby boomers to enter the system. Social Security simply cannot absorb the costs of these retirees. So if you're one of those people born after 1939, in my opinion you had better do some planning on your own.

In addition to prohibiting the baby boomers from retiring on Social Security, other changes still must be made if the system is to remain solvent (exclusive of any economic disaster). First, the automatic cost of living increases certainly will have to be curtailed, if not totally eliminated. Second, the benefits will probably be means-tested (those who have the resources will be required to pay more and receive less). Third, some method to fund the system, in addition to direct taxes, will have to be found.

It is on this last point that I would like to dwell for just a moment.

In a book I wrote in 1991, *The Coming Economic Earthquake,* I made a passing comment about an idea I believe will be used to help keep the Social Security system solvent when more tax increases are not politically feasible. This idea raised such a furor that I have tried to think it through again. And having done so, I am even more convinced it is too logical to ignore. So I would like to share my opinion about how Social Security can (and perhaps will) be funded when the crisis hits.

At present there is about $2.5 trillion in private retirement accounts of all kinds. Of this amount, much of it is held by individuals making more than $50,000 a year. Does that give you any ideas? It does me.

The possibility of private retirement accounts being "absorbed" to pay for future Social Security benefits seems too plausible to ignore, especially for higher income people and those not yet retired. The precedent already exists in the way the government is absorbing the Social Security trust funds to fund the current budget deficits.

At present the Treasury issues T-bills, which are then substituted for the funds in trust. No matter how you look at it, this is a transfer of dollars for IOUs, and virtually no one is objecting. A similar process can easily be applied to retirement accounts, when and if necessary.

If you think this is too farfetched and that our politicians would never allow this to happen, then you probably are justified in doing nothing further. But if you also believe this is a possibility, then you would be better off not placing all of your retirement funds in a tax deferred plan, even if the current tax laws allow you to do so.

I personally believe that no more than one half of what you are allowed (by law) should be tax deferred. It is my observation that any time the government allows you a tax break, they tend to think of that money as *theirs*. It would be better to pay the taxes on a portion of your long-term investment money and then invest with after-tax dollars than to run the risk of winding up with nothing but empty promises. As I said previously, this is my own opinion, which you may decide is or is not valid for yourself. Personally I would rather pay some taxes and keep my money than save some taxes and potentially lose it all.

BENEFITS

The Social Security system is very complex. It has a variety of benefits from retirement pensions to disability, each somewhat intertwined. Those who qualify for disability receive different benefits from those who do not. Widows and widowers who qualify on their spouses' incomes receive different benefits from those who earned the income personally. Those who retire at one age receive different benefits from those who retire later. And on it goes.

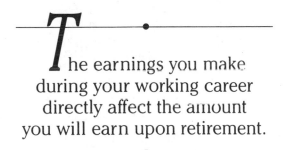

The earnings you make during your working career directly affect the amount you will earn upon retirement.

In this section I would like to break down the basic qualifications and benefits and then point you to more complete information, if you have a specific question about your own benefits.

It would be great if the Social Security Administration published a chart of earnings and benefits so retirees could just look up their total earnings, draw a line over to the benefits side, and see how much they would have at retirement, but it just can't be done.

The table on the next page is about as close as one can get but, even so, you need to understand that it will yield only a general idea of your benefits.

The only accurate way to determine exactly what your future benefits will be is to obtain an audit of your Social Security account.

A Social Security Audit

Since the earnings you make during your working career directly affect the amount you will earn upon retirement, it is important to calculate what your benefits will be for planning purposes. This is particularly true for those over age 50.

A worker is deemed to be fully "vested" or insured once he or she has paid into the system for forty quarters, with some exceptions made for those who came into the system as a result of tax law changes passed in 1984. However, since the government never makes anything simple, there are several exceptions.

A quarter for Social Security purposes is any period in which a worker earns the required amount ($540 as of 1991). So if you were paid $2,160 for any month that year, you earned four quarters worth of credit ($540 x 4 = $2,160), but you cannot accumulate more than four quarters of Social Security benefits in a single year, no matter how much you earned.

The schedule for minimum annual earnings has been increased as the Social Security tax and benefits have increased, so earlier years require less earnings, later years more.

Also, retirement benefits are adjusted for different levels of earnings, so participation in later years can enhance earnings, while nonparticipation will reduce retirement earnings.

If the accuracy of the Social Security Administration equals that of other branches of the federal government, you can expect some errors in your records. Many people have

Table for Estimating Amounts of Social Security Benefits

Average Monthly Wage	Old-Age Benefit Age 65	Old-Age Benefit Age 62	Dependent Spouse Age 65	Dependent Spouse Age 62	Average Monthly Wage	Old-Age Benefit Age 65	Old-Age Benefit Age 62	Dependent Spouse Age 65	Dependent Spouse Age 62
$83	144	115	72	54	930	618	494	309	232
92	1158	127	79	59	955	626	501	313	235
101	172	138	86	65	980	634	507	317	238
107	184	147	92	69	1000	640	512	320	240
122	195	156	105	79	1030	648	519	324	243
146	210	168	105	79	1050	654	523	327	245
169	224	179	112	84	1075	661	529	331	248
193	239	191	119	90	1100	669	535	334	251
216	253	202	127	95	1125	676	540	338	253
239	268	215	134	101	1150	683	546	341	256
258	280	224	140	105	1175	690	552	345	259
281	294	235	147	110	1200	696	557	348	261
300	306	245	153	115	1225	703	562	352	264
323	320	256	160	120	1250	710	568	355	266
342	331	265	166	124	1275	716	573	358	269
365	346	277	173	130	1300	722	578	361	271
389	361	288	180	135	1325	729	583	364	273
412	375	300	188	141	1350	735	588	367	276
436	388	311	194	146	1375	741	593	371	278
459	402	322	201	151	1400	747	597	373	280
478	413	330	206	155	1425	753	602	376	282
501	427	341	213	160	1450	759	607	379	285
524	440	352	220	165	1475	764	612	382	287
548	454	363	227	170	1500	770	616	385	289
563	464	371	232	174	1525	775	620	388	291
577	473	379	237	178	1550	781	625	390	293
591	483	387	242	181	1575	786	629	393	295
609	495	396	248	186	1600	792	635	396	297
641	517	413	258	194	1625	797	638	399	299
660	527	421	263	198	1650	803	642	401	301
685	536	429	268	201	1675	808	647	404	303
705	544	435	272	204	1700	814	651	407	305
725	551	441	276	207	1725	819	655	410	307
745	559	447	280	210	1750	825	660	412	309
770	567	454	284	213	1775	830	664	415	311
790	573	459	287	215	1800	836	669	418	313
810	580	464	290	218	1825	841	673	421	315
835	588	470	294	221	1850	847	677	423	318
860	596	477	298	223	1875	852	682	426	320
885	604	483	302	226	1900	858	686	429	322
910	611	489	306	229					

been shocked to find out that their benefits have been miscalculated due to contributions not being allocated to their accounts properly. It is extremely important to audit your Social Security file prior to retirement so you can clear up any errors if necessary. The Social Security Administration will run a free audit of your file upon request. This form is the "Request for Earnings and Benefits Statement." You can obtain one at no cost by calling your local Social Security office and requesting a copy of Form SSA-7004PC. Once you fill it out and return it, the audit normally follows in six to eight weeks and is called the "Personal Earnings and Benefit Record" (Form SSA-700PC).

After you receive the audit of your work record (and your spouse's too), you will need to review it carefully. It will show every year in which you were credited for contributions and how many credits you have earned. It will also provide an estimate of your projected retirement benefits (plus disability and survivor's benefits) and the amount by which your benefits would be reduced for early retirement. This is an excellent service provided by the Social Security Administration, and you should take advantage of it.

WHAT IF THERE IS AN ERROR?

If you don't have the hard record data (primarily tax records) to back up your claims, you can still appeal through the same process. Hopefully the IRS will still have your past tax forms and will provide them upon request, although personally I have not seen many positive examples in this area.

If your appeal is denied, you should obtain legal representation if the disputed amount justifies the additional expense. Your next step is an appeal for an administrative hearing, and you will probably need someone familiar with the process and rules of evidence within the Social Security administration.

If your internal appeal is denied (usually a one-to-two year procedure), you can still appeal to the Social Security Appeals Council in Washington, D.C. This group hears appeals based on the written evidence supplied to the Social Security Administration. It is rare for the Appeals Council to overturn a previous ruling within the administration, but you cannot appeal to the Federal courts without a ruling from the Appeals Council.

The last appeal step is in the Federal District Court. This process is usually very expensive and should not be taken without the counsel of a competent attorney who specializes in Social Security Administration law.

By the way, a 1987 study done by the Government Accounting Office (GAO) estimated that as many as nine million American workers may have errors in their work records. So check it out! If you find that your file has errors, you will need to appeal to the Social Security Administration for correction. Finding the W-2s or similar records to use in correcting the errors may not be simple. If you have not kept them, you will need to appeal to the IRS for copies.

Recently I had my own account audited through Social Security; it reflected a four-year gap in "contributions" paid into the system. Fortunately I keep all of my past income tax statements so I'm pretty certain that the records can be corrected. It has only been recently that the Social Security administration has allowed these records to be corrected beyond the statute of limitations (seven years). How long this option will remain is impossible to tell. But I would recommend that anyone not already drawing benefits request an audit immediately.

One additional factor that can affect some retirees is that illegal aliens are using Social Security numbers of U.S. citizens to draw benefits—including, and especially, disability benefits. No one really knows the extent of this fraud, but recently I talked with someone who had this happen to him.

Bill Reece was planning for his retirement from the John Deere Company after nearly thirty years of employment. The company was restructuring and offered Bill an early retirement option at age 63. Since he had plans to join a mission group that worked in Latin America, he willingly accepted. Then his nightmare began.

Bill applied for Social Security early retirement and received a notice that there was a problem with his account. After several weeks of frustration with the regional Social Security office, Bill learned that someone had been drawing disability benefits based on his Social Security record.

Bill proved to the satisfaction of the local office that he was the real William Reece who had opened the original account and had been diligently paying into it for more than forty years. But it wasn't that simple.

When the other party had applied for disability benefits, dutifully accompanied by notarized doctors' statements to that effect, the account had been transferred to the disability claims division, and the address changed. When Bill's subsequent contributions had been sent in by his employer, they apparently went into what one agent called "the La-La Land Account."

Since the government never returns any funds that can otherwise be kept for spending, the system is designed to accumulate contributions, regardless of whether the accounts balance or not. One would reasonably think the accounting system would balance all income against all applied benefits— not so, apparently.

What this meant to Bill was that since the time that someone else qualified for disability using his contributions record, none of his subsequent contributions were credited to his account. For all intents, Bill had lost nearly eight years of contributions, and since the loss involved was the last eight years of his earnings, the difference in retirement benefits was significant.

Fortunately, in Bill's case the discrepancy was recent enough that he had the tax records to correct his account. But even now he will periodically receive a bill from the Social Security Administration demanding repayment of funds he never used from the disability side—the price you pay for computers I guess.

ENTITLEMENT QUALIFICATIONS

Your Social Security entitlement is based on whether or not you have paid in enough quarters. These credits are earned by quarterly contributions to the Social Security system, based on your earnings. They are calculated on the amount you pay if you are self-employed or the amount you and your employer pay if you are an employee.

Any worker who has paid in at least the minimum for forty quarters is qualified for Social Security old age (retirement) benefits. In some cases you may actually need fewer quarters. But since that exception applies only to those who would have reached retirement age prior to 1991, I will assume if it applies to you, you already know it.

EARLY RETIREMENT

Since I covered this topic in an early chapter, I won't repeat it, except to give you the formula for calculating early retirement (from age 62 to maximum retirement age). You will lose 0.555 percent of your benefits for each month you draw benefits prior to your maximum retirement age.

For example: If you chose to retire at age 62 and you would be fully qualified at age 65, you would lose 13.333 percent of your maximum benefits (0.555 x 36 months).

WIDOWS AND WIDOWERS

The widow or widower of a fully vested worker is entitled to 100 percent of what a retired worker was receiving. Although the spouse of a deceased worker may also qualify for benefits on his or her own work history, the total benefits cannot be greater than the maximum the surviving spouse would have received either under the deceased spouse's benefits, or his or her own work record. In other words, you can't draw more than 100 percent benefits—no matter what.

Widows or widowers who apply for their deceased spouses' benefits at age 60 (earliest age, excluding a disabled child or spouse) will have their benefits reduced by 0.475 of the benefit for each month prior to age 65. For example, a widow receiving benefits at age 60 would receive only 71.5 percent of her husband's benefits.

A divorced spouse who lived with an insured worker for ten years or more is entitled to benefits under the worker's plan, beginning at age 62.

The benefits for the divorced spouse are 50 percent of the entitled worker's benefits at age 65. If the divorced spouse takes early retirement, the benefits are reduced by .722 percent for every month prior to age 65.

DISABILITY

A disabled spouse is entitled to benefits based on the worker's contribution record. This is a rather complicated formula, depending on the age of the disabled spouse. Basically the disabled spouse can start drawing benefits as young as age 50, with the benefits subject to the same rules for early retirement—a reduction of .475 percent per month prior to age 65, plus an additional reduction of .179 per month prior to age 60. Plus, the disabled spouse must be legally disabled at least five months before drawing benefits (if that doesn't confuse you, you must work for Social Security).

EMPLOYEES OF NOT-FOR-PROFIT

In 1984 the tax laws were changed to require all members of non-profit organizations to contribute to Social Security. (*Note*: ordained or licensed pastors are the exception to this rule.) As a result of this forced inclusion into the system, the rules for employees of non-profits were changed.

If you were at least 55 years of age on January 1, 1984, the following table indicates if you are fully vested in the system.

Age on January 1, 1984	Quarters of Coverage
60 or over	6
59	8
58	12
57	16
55 or 56	20

Other Income

If you have worked outside the continental United States or were previously exempt from Social Security through a state or local government exclusion, you will need to have an audit of your contribution record done to determine your exact benefits available.

How to Apply for Benefits

For those who have obtained an audit of their Social Security records and know they are correct, the next step is to apply for benefits. You will need to apply through your local Social Security office. They will provide you with all the necessary forms (see the list below). You can have the forms mailed to your home or office by calling ahead.

*T*he most important aspect of qualifying for benefits is to have all the records necessary.

Form SSA-1 F6   - Application for Retirement Insurance Benefits

Form SSA-2 F6   - Application for Wife's or Husband's Insurance Benefits

Form SSA-10BK - Application for Widow's or Widower's Insurance Benefits

Form SSA-4BK   - Application for Child's Insurance Benefits

Form SSA-5 F6   - Application for Mother's or Father's Insurance Benefits

Form SSA-8 F4   - Application for Lump-Sum Death Payment

You should apply for benefits at least three months prior to retirement. Retroactive payments can be made for only six months after qualifying for benefits, so don't delay too long or you will lose them.

You need to set up a Social Security file at home and place one copy of all your information in it. Remember to write down the names and job titles of everyone with whom you make contact. This will make future contacts much easier.

Many people have a tendency to brush aside suggestions like this but, as a counselor, I can tell you: In the event of a problem, good records are invaluable. In the event of a death they are absolutely imperative. So write it all down, and file it.

The most important aspect of qualifying for benefits is to have all the records necessary. You will need two proofs of your age (birth certificate, marriage license, Armed Services record, Bible entries—almost anything that the Social Security Department will accept).

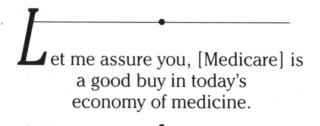

*L*et me assure you, [Medicare] is
a good buy in today's
economy of medicine.

If you are qualifying under someone else's benefits, i.e., a divorced or deceased spouse, you will need to provide notarized copies of the legal documents.

If you are qualifying for Medicare benefits, remember that you *must apply* to receive any benefits even though you will automatically be eligible at age 65. Also you do not have to be receiving Social Security retirement benefits to draw Medicare benefits.

MEDICARE PART A

Even if you do not qualify for Social Security retirement benefits, you still can apply for voluntary enrollment in the

Medicare system. As of January 1992, the cost is $177 per month for Medicare Part A benefits. Let me assure you, this is a good buy in today's economy of medicine.

Medicare Part A hospital insurance includes five categories of covered services: hospitalization, post-hospital skilled nursing facility care, post-hospital home health care, hospice care, and blood. Specific kinds of care and supplies under these general categories include the following items.

1. semiprivate room
2. meals
3. regular nursing services
4. operating and recovery room services
5. anesthesia services
6. intensive care and coronary care
7. drugs furnished by the hospital
8. laboratory tests
9. diagnostic X-rays
10. some medical supplies and appliances
11. rehabilitation services
12. preparatory services for kidney transplants
13. psychiatric care in a hospital for special cases
14. home health visits from an approved agency
15. physical therapy
16. speech therapy
17. medical social service
18. blood transfusions

MEDICARE PART B

You will automatically be eligible for Medicare Part B if you qualify for Medicare Part A (by eligibility or enrollment option). However you do not have to take the Part B coverage even if you are taking Medicare Part A.

If you are 65 you can qualify for Medicare Part B even if you don't qualify for Part A for any reason.

Medicare Part B is a fee-based system that, as of this date, costs $29.90 per month. Medical Insurance benefits cover the following general categories of services: doctor bills and other medical expenses and supplies, outpatient hospital treatment, home health care, and blood. Medical Insurance helps pay for some services and supplies that are not covered by Hospital Insurance. Under certain conditions and limitations, Medicare B also covers the following specific kinds of care and supplies:

1. ambulance transportation
2. artificial limbs and eyes
3. chiropractor's treatment for subluxation of the spine
4. oral surgery (not including ordinary dental care)
5. diagnostic testing prior to hospital stay
6. durable medical equipment, such as wheelchairs or oxygen equipment for use in the home
7. home dialysis equipment, supplies, and periodic support services
8. home and office services of independent physical therapists
9. independent laboratory tests
10. optometrist's services for fitting corrective lenses after cataract surgery
11. outpatient maintenance dialysis
12. outpatient physical therapy and speech pathology services
13. outpatient psychiatric services
14. podiatrist's services
15. surgical dressings, splints, casts, braces, and colostomy supplies
16. training for home dialysis
17. X-rays and radiation treatments
18. pap smear examinations (one every three years)
19. AIDS or AIDS-related complex, provided disability requirements are met[1]

I reiterate: This is a good value by any measure. The equivalent commercial coverage would probably cost more than

---

1. From *The Complete & Easy Guide to Social Security & Medicare, 1991 Edition,* by Faustin F. Jehle, Fraser Publishing Company. Used by permission.

$100 a month and, in some cases, such as pre-existing conditions, other coverage may not be available at any price.

EARNED VERSUS UNEARNED INCOME

Social Security retirement benefits are calculated on the basis of what the Social Security Administration considers *earned income*—money you were paid for doing a job. If you work for someone else, your *gross* wages—everything you earn before anything is deducted—are counted as earned income. If you are self-employed, the calculations are made on your *net* income—what's left after expenses are deducted. Some other sources of income are considered *unearned,* are not included in your income calculation for Social Security purposes, and do not affect the amount of your benefits. (Though these exempt categories are not counted in calculating benefits, many of them are subject to federal taxation.)

EARNED INCOME

The money you earn for your work counts toward your benefits. If you are employed, your employer or employers report your work, deduct your Social Security taxes, and file a W-2 form. You should get a copy of the W-2 form from each employer early in the year following the year in which you worked. If you are a self-employed person, you pay your own Social Security taxes when you complete your quarterly income tax returns and send them in.

ITEMS COUNTED AS EARNED INCOME

When you count your earned income, you should include any of the following items. These items are considered earned income, and count toward getting retirement benefits.

1. Wages
2. Cash tips of $20 or more a month

3. Wages in kind—room and board unless you are a household (domestic) worker or a farm worker or you perform services that are not in the course of your employer's trade or business
4. Bonuses
5. Commissions
6. Fees
7. Vacation pay
8. Pay in lieu of (instead of) vacation
9. Severance pay
10. Sick pay

ITEMS NOT COUNTED AS EARNED INCOME

The following items are *not* considered earned income. They do not count toward credits for retirement benefits. If you are already receiving retirement benefits, these exempt earnings do not affect those benefits.

1. Dividends
2. Savings bank interest
3. Bond interest
4. Income from Social Security benefits
5. Veterans Administration benefits
6. Pension/retirement plan income
7. Annuities
8. Sale of capital assets
9. Gifts
10. Inheritances
11. Rental income
12. Royalties received after you are age 65 from patents or copyrights granted before the year in which you became 65
13. Retirement payments from a partnership under a written agreement
14. Income from a limited partnership—that income is deemed an investment
15. Income from self-employment received in any year after the year in which you become entitled to retire-

ment benefits, as long as that income is not gained from services rendered after the date of retirement.

16. Jury fees
17. Wages or other income accrued for services rendered in years prior to the year in which you become entitled to retirement benefits, as long as that income is not gained from services rendered in the years of retirement.

Delayed Retirement Credit for Work After 65

If you continue working after 65, and if you do not collect retirement benefits, you will receive a DRC (Delayed Retirement Credit). This is additional credit toward your Social Security benefits when you do retire. The following additional credits apply.

1. If you turned 65 in 1981 or earlier, your benefit would be increased 1 percent for each year you continue to work after age 65 and up to age 70.
2. If you turned 64 in 1982 or later, the credit is increased to 3 percent a year for each additional year you delay retirement.
3. Beginning in 1990, DRC will increase an additional 1/2 of 1 percent every other year for workers reaching 66 after 2008. The DRC applies only to the worker's personal benefit, not to dependents. It does apply, however, to the widow's or widower's benefit.

The Only Forms You Need for Reporting Income

If you are employed after age 65, you must send to the Social Security Administration your income and tax statements: Social Security Form (SSA-7770 F6) and IRS Form W-2.

Excess Earnings

If you were *over* 70 years of age for the entire year of 1983, or any year thereafter, you can earn income of any amount without affecting your benefits.

If you are *under* 70 years of age and earned over the exempt amount, benefits are affected. Here are the 1991 figures.

1991	*Annual*	*Monthly*
65 or over	$9,720	$810
Under 65	7,080	590

If you earn more than the exempt amount, then $1 in benefits is withheld for each $3 you earn over the exempt amount while you are 65 to 69.

Your Social Security Income

You should be aware of the following rules and procedures concerning your income.

1. *Separate checks:* A husband and wife who are living together may receive one check made out to both of them, but separate checks will be sent if requested.

2. *Overpayments, mispayments:* Overpayments will be withheld from the next checks. If there is a conflict between what Social Security says you should repay and your figures, take your records to your local Social Security office.

3. *For your protection:* You should know that Social Security checks cannot be assigned for payment to someone else and are not subject to levy, garnishment, or attachment, except in very restricted situations, such as collection of federal taxes or by court order to child support or alimony.

4. *Delivery to a representative:* If you fill out a form at your Social Security office, your checks, made out in your name, will be mailed to anyone you designate. You still have to endorse and cash or deposit them.

5. *Direct deposit to a bank:* You can have your check sent directly to your bank for automatic deposit.

Note: Before you decide to use direct deposit, check on your bank's policies. Some banks charge for this service. Other banks will not and may offer other special help, such as notifying you when your check arrives. You should also make sure that the bank will forward any communications to you the bank receives from the Social Security Administration.[2]

*I*f you have worked
the required number of quarters in a
job where Social Security taxes were
withheld, you can qualify for some
level of benefits.

CHAPTER FOURTEEN

Military, Ministers, and Missionaries

MILITARY RETIREES

Those who retire from the military have a special set of conditions unlike virtually any other group. They are usually retired at a much younger age than other career fields (average age 42) and have benefits unique to only military retirees. The use of military commissaries, military health care facilities, and the opportunity to start a second career in their forties make these retirees truly unique.

In my opinion we will see many of the benefits for military retirees curtailed in future years as government revenues are stretched thinner. There is no logic to retiring so many people at the peak of their work career. Military retirement is a good deal for those who are already in it, but there is simply no way the country can afford the system. It was designed around the needs of military personnel who fought for their country during extended periods of war. These benefits were but small payments by a grateful nation to its soldiers, and rightly so. But the need is past and, in my opinion, the costs are simply too high.

*Y*our eligibility for CHAMPUS ends the day you *qualify* for Medicare Part A—regardless of whether you apply for Medicare or not.

I don't want to demean anyone living on military retirement. You paid the price and the nation has a contractual agreement with you that it should keep. But be aware: In our situational ethic society, vows are a thing to be kept only when convenient. As the economy continues to run down, it will eventually be seen as an option, not a contract.

CHAMPUS Coverage

The Civilian Health and Medical Program of the U.S. (CHAMPUS) covers the health care needs of military retirees and their dependents until the retiree qualifies for Medicare Part A, at which time the retiree and his or her dependents are no longer eligible for CHAMPUS.

This is an important factor since your eligibility for CHAMPUS ends the day you *qualify* for Medicare Part A—regardless of whether you apply for Medicare or not. So you can have an inadvertent gap in coverage if you do not file for Medicare benefits.

CHAMPUS is a comprehensive medical benefits plan that in many ways is very similar to Medicare Parts A and B, except that CHAMPUS users are eligible for treatment in military hospitals where available.

There is no annual fee for CHAMPUS, although there is a 25 percent deductible charge on usual and ordinary services, such as doctor visits and hospital care. I won't attempt to cover all the various aspects of CHAMPUS. You can obtain a copy of the CHAMPUS handbook from any military hospital or by writing CHAMPUS, Aurora, CO 80045-6900.

One last note of caution: If you are eligible for Medicare Part A at age 65, you *must* file for it since your CHAMPUS coverage stops at midnight the day you turn 65. If you are not eligible for Medicare, you must get a disallowance notice from the local Social Security Department office to ensure that your CHAMPUS will continue.

*S*ocial Security credits toward retirement benefits may be received for military service in any of the Armed Forces.

If you are a retired reservist, you can qualify for CHAMPUS coverage at age 60. But the same rules regarding Medicare apply to you at age 65, so be sure to apply for Medicare if you qualify.

VETERANS

If you became employed after leaving military service and you paid Social Security taxes on the maximum earnings, the information below may not be pertinent to your benefits. However this information may be important if you did not work on a regular basis or if you worked very little, either because of illness or because of lack of technical skills. This information also may be important to your spouse or children.

Farmers, household (domestic) workers, and self-employed non-regular workers who have had military service also may need this information. Their military service credits may be important to them and their families in applying for Social Security benefits.

ENTITLEMENT TO CREDITS

Social Security credits toward retirement benefits may be received for military service in any of the Armed Forces.

If you were in active military service between 1940 and 1956, you are entitled to one quarter of Social Security coverage for each calendar quarter you were in active service, if your discharge was under conditions other than dishonorable. Dishonorable discharge entitles you to no credits.

For each month you were in active service you are credited $160, even though no Social Security taxes were paid during the period 1940 to 1956. These wage credits are not payable as a separate benefit. They are used, if needed, to establish insured status or to increase your benefit. No determination as to the use of military service wage credits can be made until an application for benefits is filed.

After January 1, 1957, Social Security taxes were withheld. You are required to prove your period of active service during any time from 1940 to the date of leaving the service in order for you to obtain all the credits to which you are entitled.

PROOF REQUIREMENTS

Proof of your age at the time of entering military service, your date of birth, and the record of your military service are essential to any claim for credits. You should request a certified copy of your military record from the Armed Forces.

ARMED FORCES DISABILITY BENEFITS

If you are receiving military retirement pay from the Armed Forces because of disability, and not based on length of service, you are entitled also to credits for Social Security benefits covering the same time period. This is very important to veterans of the Korean conflict and Vietnam. You may be entitled to Social Security disability benefits *in addition* to your Armed Forces disability retirement benefits.

RESTRICTIONS ON WORK CREDITS

If you get credit toward military retirement benefits for military service from any of the Armed Forces, the Social Security Administration will not give you any work credits toward Social Security benefits covering the same time period. Exceptions are noted as follows.

EXCEPTIONS

If the benefit is paid by the Veterans Administration, the Social Security Administration will give you credits.

If you are a "length of service" retiree from the Armed Forces and rendered active duty service between 1951 and 1956 and were on active duty service after 1956, you can receive credits for Social Security for each quarter during such period if another federal agency also is not using this same period of time to compute an annuity.

If you are a widower, you can get credit for certain military service. Under certain circumstances widowers are permitted to waive the right to a civil service survivor's annuity and receive credit (not otherwise possible) for military service prior to 1957 for purposes of determining eligibility for, and the amount of, Social Security survivors' benefits. Under former law, only widows were allowed to exercise this option. The new law is effective and, with respect to monthly benefits, payable for months after the month of enactment.

For individual assistance contact the Retiree Affairs office in the Personnel Section at the nearest military base or the Military Personnel Center for the specific branch of service from which the person retired. These are trained specialists who will help with the details of military retirement pay and CHAMPUS insurance without fee.

Access to military records is restricted to the veteran himself or herself, next of kin if the veteran is deceased, federal officers for official purposes, or those with release authorization signed by the veteran or his or her next of kin. The form that must be submitted for this information is Request Pertaining to Military Records, #180; it gives all the addresses of the records depositories for the different services. To obtain this form, write to: National Personnel Records Center, 9700 Page Blvd, St. Louis, MO 63132.[1]

MINISTERS AND MISSIONARIES

Prior to 1984, employees of non-profit organizations were exempt from Social Security if the organization they worked for elected not to be covered. The 1984 Tax Act brought these organizations under the Social Security Act, as well as all of their employees.

In 1986 the law was modified again to allow religious organizations (and some religious orders) to be exempt from the system if they so elected, but all employees are still required to contribute to the Social Security system. Effectively the organization is exempt, but the employees are not. Somehow this seems to make sense in Washington, if nowhere else.

In addition, ministers of the gospel are allowed to opt out of Social Security on grounds of religious conviction. In other words, they have to object to government-sponsored welfare.

As a result of these law changes and previous exemptions, there are many retired pastors and their families who are not covered by Social Security benefits today.

Although the wages earned by a pastor may have been exempt from Social Security, any wages earned through other sources of income (royalties or other jobs) were, and still are, subject to Social Security taxes.

If you have worked the required number of quarters in a job where Social Security taxes were withheld, you can qualify for some level of benefits.

One note of admonishment: if you opted out of the Social Security system for conscientious reasons, you need to test your motives for seeking coverage later. If the decision was one of economic convenience, the motive was wrong. Literally

1. Information adapted from *The Complete & Easy Guide to Social Security & Medicare, 1991 Edition,* by Faustin Jehle, Fraser Publishing Company. Used by permission.

once you signed Form 4361, asking to be removed from the Social Security system, you made a vow and you should keep that vow, irrespective of any financial gain. Even though the income you earned from other sources was subject to Social Security taxes (a circumstance you could not control) that in no way negates your vow.

If I could encourage active pastors and missionaries in the area of housing, it would be to purchase a home well in advance of retirement.

Remember what Solomon said about vows we make, *"When you make a vow to God, do not be late in paying it, for He takes no delight in fools. Pay what you vow! It is better that you should not vow than that you should vow and not pay"* (Ecclesiastes 5:4-5).

Retired Ministers' and Missionaries' Housing

The availability of church-provided housing was a blessing to many ministers and missionaries during their working careers, but it can be become a source of financial frustration after retirement. Often they are thrust into an overpriced housing market with far less income than even the average retiree who either owns a home or is at least buying one from a less expensive time period.

If I could encourage active pastors and missionaries in the area of housing, it would be to purchase a home well in advance of retirement. Even a rental home will normally maintain pace with the average inflation rate.

If you are retired and do not own a home, I would offer some advice and some encouragement.

First, the advice. Try to purchase a home, condo, or mobile home that is within your budget (described in the next chapter). If you cannot buy a home within your budget (no more than 40 percent of your income after tithe and taxes), you're better off renting.

Now the word of encouragement. If you have been serving the Lord in your career to the best of your ability, God has obligated Himself to meet your needs (as opposed to wants and desires). Pray diligently, share your needs with other believers, and claim God's promise: *"Offer to God a sacrifice of thanksgiving, and pay your vows to the Most High; and call upon Me in the day of trouble; I shall rescue you, and you will honor Me"* (Psalm 50:14-15).

God can and does answer the prayers of His faithful servants. I recently witnessed two practical examples of God's provision. A dear Christian brother who pastored a church in Arkansas recently retired with a very small pension to supplement his Social Security. In his last years in the small church he and his wife purchased a modest home that stretched their budget to the limit. After retirement it was woefully beyond their budget.

They struggled to keep the house for nearly two years after retiring, while sacrificing virtually all other necessities. Even with both of them working part time they were constantly strapped to make the payments and pay the taxes and upkeep.

At their request I reviewed their budget, and my advice was painfully simple: Sell your home. You can't afford it. After praying and seeking other counsel, they put the home up for sale. It sold quickly and they netted about $20,000, which they were able to keep by using their one-time housing exemption.

But there they were with $20,000, a limited income, and facing a rental market that was more expensive than their past mortgage payment. Then one day, before they had even moved from their home, the pastor received a call from a member of a church he had pastored for several years in another state.

"Pastor," the caller said, "we heard that you had retired and several of us you ministered to when you were here got together and decided we'd like to do something for you and your wife."

While telling me about it the pastor could hardly contain himself. This church, which knew absolutely nothing about his plight, had taken up a collection of $40,000. With his $20,000 and the gift of $40,000, he and his wife purchased a very nice, double-wide mobile home on a beautiful lot—for cash.

God knew his need long before he retired and planned adequately for it. And, by the way, my friend continues to minister as a volunteer counselor to this day.

Recently an ex-pastor I know moved to a western state where ultimately he and his wife would like to retire. They had long desired to buy a home, but they could never afford to do so. One night, a few weeks before they were to relocate, he sat up in bed, shook his wife awake, and said, "I just remembered that I had an annuity with our church in Ohio."

His wife grunted, "That was thirty years ago. We haven't talked to anyone there in twenty years."

He went back to sleep, but the next day he called the church and talked to the treasurer, asking if he knew anything about the ancient annuity.

"No," he replied, "but I'll call the previous treasurer and ask if he does."

The next day the treasurer called back and reported, "Your annuity is still in force and you have a little more than $40,000 accumulated. Where would you like to have it sent?"

God does care about the needs of His people, and as the old cliché goes, "Seldom early, but never late."

*M*anage what you have, trust that God is true to His Word and, in response to your stewardship, He will supply what is needed later.

CHAPTER FIFTEEN

A Retiree's Budget

As important as making the right investment decisions is, there is nothing more important to a retiree than learning to live on a budget. The errors in spending that you may have made while fully employed were probably nuisances. But those you make while living on a retirement income can easily become disasters of the first magnitude.

Recently I counseled with a couple who learned a hard lesson about budgeting. The husband had retired the previous year from IBM where he had accepted early retirement as a part of the company's cost reduction moves. He had received his retirement of $275,000 as a lump sum, and with this much money available to supplement his Social Security income at age 62, the couple assumed they would have no financial problems.

The wife, Anne, said, "I guess we should have realized that we couldn't do the same things we had done when Ben was working, but we didn't realize how difficult it would be to decrease our spending level. Our spending has declined some, but not in the same ratio as our income. For the first time in our lives, we're going into debt every month."

*Y*ou must agree *together* to live on a budget in which every expense for the entire year is allocated and funded.

They had come in to ask if they should take some of their retirement savings and pay off their credit card debts to save on the interest they were paying. This is a common question with a simple answer, and I told them *they should, but not until some prerequisites are met first*.

1. The cause of the overspending must first be corrected or else the consolidation (which is the equivalent of what they were proposing) will be temporary at best.
2. There must be an absolute commitment to no more credit card debt (or any other consumer debt). There are three basic rules for using a credit card that are absolutes for retirees.
   a. Never use credit cards except as a temporary substitute for cash.
   b. Pay the balance off every month—no matter what!
   c. The first month you find that you cannot pay off the credit cards out of allocated income, destroy them and vow to use them no more—period! Credit cards arc not the problem; the misuse of them is.
3. You must agree *together* to live on a budget in which every expense for the entire year is allocated and funded. Of necessity, this will restrict your financial freedom, just as living within your means always does, but the end result will be well worth it.

For retirees who have never tried budgeting before, it will not be an easy task, but it is necessary. For those who have regularly gotten into financial trouble, even while working full time, it is absolutely crucial. For others, it is good stewardship of your God-given resources. As Proverbs 27:23-24 says, *"Know well the condition of your flocks, and pay attention to your herds; for riches are not forever, nor does a crown endure to all generations."*

A budget should not be drudgery; it should be both simple and freeing.

After doing financial counseling for about twenty years, I can say with some degree of certainty that usually at least one half of a couple does *not* like to budget. Some people argue that a budget is too confining; others say they think too much planning shows a lack of faith, still others are more honest and admit, "I just don't like to do it."

I also know that more often than not it is the husband who does not want to budget. And since more women buy and read books than men do, I assume the majority of my readers are women. If you're the budgeter, you need to do a good selling job on the need to budget. (The same can be said for the husband of a non-conforming wife).

There are some good ways to approach the subject of budgeting with a spouse, but there are some guaranteed losers. Examples are:

You really need this.
You're always spending more than we make.
Larry Burkett says you need to learn to live on a budget.
Are you going to live on a budget or not?
I can't believe you're so stupid with money!

All of these are sure to stir up strife and detract from the basic principle: God wants us to be good stewards of what He has given us to manage. Try to approach the subject from the perspective of God's Word and good common sense. A budget should not be drudgery; it should be both simple and freeing. I can absolutely assure you that it can be because I have seen many people freed as a result of living on a good budget.

WHAT IS A BUDGET?

First, a budget will not solve your financial problems. The most any budget can do is to help you establish *self-discipline.* If there is no desire for self-discipline, the best budget in the world is doomed to failure.

Also, if there is not a commitment on the part of *both* husband and wife to work together, no financial plan will work. Rather than take up space discussing how to deal with an un-cooperative spouse, I'll point you to an earlier book entitled *Debt-Free Living,* in which this topic is discussed and alternatives are presented. In truth, though, there is no magical formula. Unless both husband and wife are willing to work together, there is no way to budget effectively.

*T*he purpose of any budget,
short range or long range,
is to balance income and outgo.

The "one size fits all" strategy does not apply to a budget. To be effective, any budget must be adapted to each family's needs. For instance, if you have $3,000 a month to budget, your need to control spending is probably down to the $20 to $50 per month level; but someone living on $800 a month needs to control spending down to $5 a month. Obviously one could argue that both income levels need to control spending down to $1 per month but, in practical truth, any attempt to do so will usually result in frustration and, ultimately, no budget at all.

BUDGETING BASICS

Before presenting the details of a budget, I would like to discuss the *concept* of budgeting. If you can first understand how a good budget works, the process of applying it to your own finances is simple.

The purpose of any budget, short range or long range, is to balance income and outgo. The larger the income, the more surplus that can be generated if expenses are held constant. Perhaps that's too simplistic for some, but you would be amazed how complicated some people try to make the budgeting process.

The less complicated a budget can be made, the more useful it is. Usually in any family at least one person is a "detailist" (a perfectionist) who wants infinite detail and, consequently, tries to account for everything, down to the last penny. For the majority of people this is unnecessary. To maintain a budget that will account for 98 percent of all spending should normally take one hour per month (maximum). To account for the other 2 percent will take at least an additional two to three hours of bookkeeping.

Too often the other side is the "generalist"—someone who wants to spend one hour per *year* keeping records. This type of person normally maintains a checking account that is so out of balance it requires $500 in reserve just to ensure that no checks bounce. The budget (if it can be so termed) consists of juggling accounts to pay the totally unexpected bills, such as annual insurance premiums, property tax bills, or late notices on the unpaid utilities. If this plan works at all, it is only because the generalist makes enough money to be sloppy and gets away with it. That won't work well for those in retirement.

Most other people are somewhere in between the detailist and the generalist. They keep their checking accounts "kind of" in balance—meaning they usually have to make an adjusting entry after two months of imbalance, because by then they're sure the bank statement is accurate. And although they're rarely late on any payments, there is usually a nagging feeling that there are unplanned expenses looming out there somewhere.

When I began doing financial counseling several years ago, it was obvious that I needed a way to communicate some simple budgeting concepts to people who had never really grasped the concept of how to maintain their checkbooks properly. I visited most of the local bookstores searching for good materials. What I found were so-called budget books written by accountants—primarily *for* accountants. If most of the people I was counseling could have understood those budget books, they wouldn't have needed my help in the first place. So I went back to the basics and designed a budget system for non-budgeters.

Think of a budget the way our parents or grandparents did before there were checking accounts. Often the money to pay bills, buy food, and replace worn clothing was kept in jars—usually hidden away somewhere in the kitchen.

I have a friend in her eighties who budgets this way. She has a note on the outside of each of her budget jars, which details how much she should reserve out of every Social Security check. One jar contains her monthly allocation for food; one is for utilities; another is for rent; another for tithe, and so on. She has developed a basic budget, and for her, it works: She knows the average monthly amount each budget category needs and, after payments are made, her jars tell her if she has any money left over.

There are some obvious improvements she could make to her budget, such as allocations for non-monthly expenses— medical expenses, car repairs, and travel. But these are just refinements of the basic concept and are simple to make after the basics of budgeting are understood.

Many times in working with families I have actually used an envelope budgeting system to get them started. I normally use at least twelve envelopes to cover the major categories.

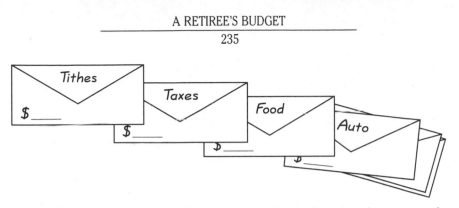

On the outside of each envelope I write how much should be put in per pay period. This is done to help balance income and outgo, since normally they are not perfectly matched by pay period. It may be necessary to shift some expenses, such as food and car repairs, to the second pay period since the mortgage or rent payments normally fall in the first pay period.

Some expenses don't fall due every month, but it is essential to allocate some funds to these expenses. Those who don't are often fooled into thinking they have extra money at the end of a month, when actually what they have are bills that haven't come due. For instance, you don't have to buy tires for your car every month, but eventually you must, so some allocation each month for tire replacement lessens the burden when they finally wear out.

Another such expense is dental care. Dental bills don't occur every month for most people, but eventually most people need some dental work. If your average cost for dental care is $600 a year, common sense says that $50 a month should be put in reserve for this eventual need. So within the budget's medical expense envelope, a portion of the cash reserve would be "dental work."

If in any single month you have a special need, such as an abnormally expensive car repair, it is possible to borrow from another envelope, such as the "medical expenses" if there is a surplus. But by doing so you make a conscious decision to postpone your medical or dental care.

All any budget can do is make you *think* about your spending and evaluate the consequences that any one spending decision has on all the others. If you find yourself robbing envelopes regularly, you either need to increase your income or reduce your expenses.

Obviously most Americans, including retirees, are not going to keep their household money in jars or envelopes; nor should they. But the same basic concept can be carried over to a checking account.

Instead of looking at the funds in your checking account as a lump sum, look at the total amount divided into smaller amounts that belong to the different budget categories—just like the jars or envelopes. But instead of jars or envelopes we'll use account sheets. These account sheets will show how much of the total in checking should be allocated per category.

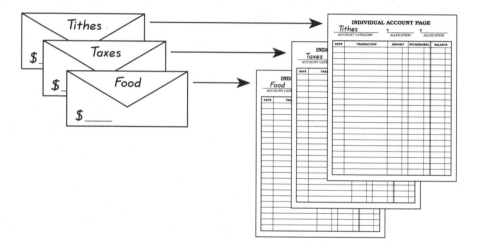

Now instead of looking in your checkbook ledger to see how much money you have left each month, you look at the account sheet for the category of spending.

Let's assume in this case you need to buy some clothes. Based on the checkbook balance, you might be tempted to spend up to $670.

CHECKBOOK LEDGER

DATE	CK. #	TRANSACTION	DEPOSIT	WITHDRAWAL	BALANCE
4-22	1232	Bargain Shoes		32 89	1081 66
4-23	1233	PD Grocery		74 20	1007 46
4-24	1234	Power Co.		165 50	841 96
4-25	1235	MCI		24 54	817 42
4-25	1236	Dr. Smith		45 00	772 42
4-26	1237	PD Grocery		12 94	759 48
4-26	1238	Sears		14 48	745 00
4-27	1239	Hank's Gym		65 00	680 00
4-28	1240	Post Office		10 00	670 00

However, a quick look at your clothing account sheet shows you actually have saved $215 for clothes.

INDIVIDUAL ACCOUNT PAGE

Clothing

ACCOUNT CATEGORY $ _____ ALLOCATION $ _____ ALLOCATION

DATE	TRANSACTION	DEPOSIT	WITHDRAWAL	BALANCE
4-17	Bargain Shoes		32 89	444 34
4-17	Joe's Fashions		64 20	380 14
4-17	Sears		47 50	332 64
4-20	Walmart		48 54	284 10
4-22	Macys		30 98	253 12
4-22	Bargain Shoes		23 64	229 48
4-26	Sears		14 48	215 00

If you decide to spend more than what your clothing account balance shows, you'll need to transfer some funds from another category. By deciding to spend more than is budgeted for clothes, you make a decision that will result in lower spending elsewhere (or else you'll live to regret spending too much on clothing).

I hope this brief explanation of how a budget works is clear because living on a budget is both biblical (good stewardship) and practical (regardless of your income).

I have often heard people say, "Why, I just don't make enough money to budget." That's nonsense. We all make enough money to budget—some more, some less. The Lord said in Luke 16:10, *"He who is faithful in a very little thing is faithful also in much; and he who is unrighteous in a very little thing is unrighteous also in much."*

Manage what you have, trust that God is true to His Word and, in response to your stewardship, He will supply what is needed later.

I have provided some sample pages from the *Financial Planning Workbook,* published by Moody Press. This is the basic information I use in all of my budget counseling. Moody also offers the *Financial Planning Organizer,* which contains a notebook, divider tabs, and all the forms necessary to develop a budget for at least one full year. You can find a copy in your local Christian bookstore, or you can write to Moody Press, 820 N. LaSalle Blvd., Chicago, IL 60610-3284.

For you detailists, we also offer a computerized version of the budget system that will balance your checkbook, as well as maintain your budget *to the penny every month,* without you having to invest the extra hours to do it. This computer program is also available at your local bookstore or from Moody Press.

Monthly Income and Expenses

GROSS INCOME PER MONTH _____

    Salary _____

    Interest _____

    Dividends _____

    Other _____

LESS:

1. **Tithe** _____

2. **Tax (Est. - Incl. Fed., State, FICA)** _____

    NET SPENDABLE INCOME _____

3. **Housing** _____

    Mortgage (rent) _____

    Insurance _____

    Taxes _____

    Electricity _____

    Gas _____

    Water _____

    Sanitation _____

    Telephone _____

    Maintenance _____

    Other _____

4. **Food** _____

5. **Automobile(s)** _____

    Payments _____

    Gas & Oil _____

    Insurance _____

    License/Taxes _____

    Maint./Repair/Replace _____

6. **Insurance** _____

    Life _____

    Medical _____

    Other _____

7. **Debts** _____

    Credit Card _____

    Loans & Notes _____

    Other _____

8. **Enter. & Recreation** _____

    Eating Out _____

    Baby Sitters _____

    Activities/Trips _____

    Vacation _____

    Other _____

9. **Clothing** _____

10. **Savings** _____

11. **Medical Expenses** _____

    Doctor _____

    Dentist _____

    Drugs _____

    Other _____

12. **Miscellaneous** _____

    Toiletry, cosmetics _____

    Beauty, barber _____

    Laundry, cleaning _____

    Allowances, lunches _____

    Subscriptions _____

    Gifts (incl. Christmas) _____

    Cash _____

    Other _____

13. **School/Child Care** _____

    Tuition _____

    Materials _____

    Transportation _____

    Day Care _____

14. **Investments** _____

    TOTAL EXPENSES _____

INCOME VS. EXPENSES

    Net Spendable Income _____

    Less Expenses _____

15. **Unallocated Surplus Income** [1] _____

[1] This category is used when surplus income is received. This would be kept in the checking account to be used within a few weeks; otherwise, it should be transferred to an allocated category.

Individual Account Page

ACCOUNT CATEGORY		$ ALLOCATION		$ ALLOCATION	

DATE	TRANSACTION	DEPOSIT	WITHDRAWAL	BALANCE

Variable Expense Planning

Plan for those expenses that are not paid on a regular monthly basis by estimating the yearly cost and determining the monthly amount needed to be set aside for that expense. A helpful formula is to allow the previous year's expense and add 5 percent.

		Estimated Cost	**Per Month**
1.	VACATION	$_____ $\div$ 12 =	$ _____
2.	DENTIST	$_____ $\div$ 12 =	$ _____
3.	DOCTOR	$_____ $\div$ 12 =	$ _____
4.	AUTOMOBILE	$_____ $\div$ 12 =	$ _____
5.	ANNUAL INSURANCE	$_____ $\div$ 12 =	$ _____
	(Life)	($_____ $\div$ 12 =	$ _____)
	(Health)	($_____ $\div$ 12 =	$ _____)
	(Auto)	($_____ $\div$ 12 =	$ _____)
	(Home)	($_____ $\div$ 12 =	$ _____)
6.	CLOTHING	$_____ $\div$ 12 =	$ _____
7.	INVESTMENTS	$_____ $\div$ 12 =	$ _____
8.	OTHER	$_____ $\div$ 12 =	$ _____
		$_____ $\div$ 12 =	$ _____

Budget Percentage Guidelines

Salary for guideline = _____ /year [1]

Gross Income Per Month _____

   1. **Tithe**   (__ % of Gross) (_____) = $ _____

   2. **Tax**   (__ % of Gross) (_____) = $ _____

Net Spendable Income   _____

   3. **Housing**   (__ % of Net) (_____) = $ _____

   4. **Food**   (__ % of Net) (_____) = $ _____

   5. **Auto**   (__ % of Net) (_____) = $ _____

   6. **Insurance**   (__ % of Net) (_____) = $ _____

   7. **Debts**   (__ % of Net) (_____) = $ _____

   8. **Entertain. & Rec.**   (__ % of Net) (_____) = $ _____

   9. **Clothing**   (__ % of Net) (_____) = $ _____

 10. **Savings**   (__ % of Net) (_____) = $ _____

 11. **Medical**   (__ % of Net) (_____) = $ _____

 12. **Miscellaneous** (__ % of Net) (_____) = $ _____

 13. **School/ Child Care**   (__ % of Net) (_____) = $ _____

 14. **Investments**   (__ % of Net) (_____) = $ _____

Total   **(Cannot exceed Net Spendable Income)** $ _____

 15. **Unallocated Surplus Income**   (__N/A__) = $ _____

[1] Refer to page 29 for percentage guidelines.

Income Allocation

		INCOME SOURCE/PAY PERIOD			
INCOME					
BUDGET CATEGORY	**MONTHLY ALLOCATION**				
1. TITHE					
2. TAX					
3. HOUSING					
4. FOOD					
5. AUTO					
6. INSURANCE					
7. DEBTS					
8. ENTERTAINMENT & RECREATION					
9. CLOTHING					
10. SAVINGS					
11. MEDICAL/DENTAL					
12. MISCELLANEOUS					
13. SCHOOL/ CHILD CARE					
14. INVESTMENTS					
15. UNALLOCATED SURPLUS INCOME					

*N*ot planning for after-death asset distribution is poor stewardship. . . A small amount of time and money invested now can result in a huge savings in time, money, and grief (for your loved ones) later.

CHAPTER SIXTEEN

Estate Planning for Retirees

ARE WILLS NECESSARY?

Most people, retirees included, don't like to discuss death, so they delay talking about it until it's too late. And if they die without a will, no one, including their spouses, can make one for them.

If you die without a valid will (or trust), the state in which you lived will decide how the assets of your estate are distributed, which may be totally contrary to what you personally would have chosen. Therefore, if you want things done your way, make a will as soon as possible; none of us knows what the future holds.

Additional hardship may result for your loved ones who are handicapped (or become so) if you die without a will or trust. Having your lifelong spouse placed in an institution may be the last thing on your mind, but that could happen if the decision is left to the state.

Some couples argue that they don't need a will because all their possessions are in joint ownership with right of survivorship. True, joint ownership with right of survivorship will transfer property to the surviving spouse automatically at the death of the first spouse. But if both spouses die at the same time, such as in a auto accident, there will be no surviving joint owner to inherit the property. Without wills, the estate distribution will be decided by the state, none of which will go to God's work.

WHO NEEDS A WILL?

Mention the word estate and most people think of the wealthy who live in elaborate homes with servants and well-manicured lawns but, according to the law, virtually everyone has an estate. Some are large; others are small. Your estate consists of everything you own. Cars, furniture, antiques, jewelry, savings accounts, and even books are considered a part of your estate. Many people have larger estates than they realize when things like retirement benefits, life insurance policies, and homes are added up. And remember that the value of your estate is not what you paid for those things; it's their fair market value at the time of your death. With the current value of land, houses, and even furniture, it's entirely possible for retirees with average means to have an estate worth hundreds of thousands of dollars.

A common comment about wills is, "I don't need one; I'm not worth enough." That's poor stewardship of what God has entrusted to a Christian. Whatever you're worth, it should be managed well.

WHAT ARE THE REQUIREMENTS FOR PREPARING A WILL?

For a will to be valid, it must meet the legal requirements of your state of primary residence. The process of determining a will's validity is called *probate,* which means to prove or to testify. Legal requirements for valid wills can vary from state to state so you should have your will reviewed by a competent attorney to be certain it complies with the laws of the state in which you live.

It's a good idea to review your will on a regular basis —certainly any time your circumstances change substantially. Periodically, ask your attorney if there are new federal or state laws that would require your will to be updated.

In order to probate a will, the original copy must be delivered to the court. For that reason, the original copy should be kept in a safe location, such as your attorney's office or maintained in a secure file with other important papers. A note in your home files should indicate where the original copy is stored. It's also good to keep a copy of the will handy for future reference.

Changing circumstances may require an update of your will.

Many people place their original wills in a safe deposit box. Depending on the state in which you live, your bank officer may be allowed to enter the box after your death and search for your will. Other states may have more strict guidelines for entering safe deposit boxes. If you live in one of those states, you will need to authorize another person to enter the box. Otherwise, a court order may be needed to enter it, which could delay the probate process. Furthermore, if no one knows about your safe deposit box, it may be impossible to locate the will.

DO IT YOURSELF?

A question often asked is, "Can I do my own will, or do I need an attorney?" The law allows a person to prepare his or her own will. One example is a *holographic* will, which must be entirely in the handwriting of the person drafting it.

However, if you draft your own will, you may be increasing the risk of it being contested or declared invalid. What's worse, if you do it wrong, it's too late to correct it after you die.

Will kits (which are fill-in-blanks wills), available in most bookstores, are another option for preparing your own will. A will "kit" generally is accepted in most states, particularly if the kit uses computer software to generate the will.

With a computerized will kit the will can be printed out, which reduces the possibility of errors. Be certain to verify the validity of will kits in your state by checking with your local probate court. It's also a good idea to have your will reviewed by a competent attorney. An hour of an attorney's time may well save your estate (and your heirs) thousands of dollars and a lot if inconvenience.

WILL UPDATES

As I mentioned before, changing circumstances may require an update of your will. If this occurs, it is not necessary to make an entirely new will. Instead, these changes could be made through the use of a *codicil,* or supplement. The codicil is subject to the same laws of probate as the will, so it must be drafted properly, and only the original is valid in court. Attach all codicils to the original will and store them together. If you have previous wills in existence, you should specify that your latest will or codicil supersedes all previous drafts.

WITNESSES

The laws for validating a will vary from state to state, usually requiring two or more witnesses. It is a good idea to use more witnesses than required by law, just in case one or more of the witnesses have died or cannot be located when your will is probated. It is also a good idea to use witnesses you know so they can be located if necessary. If your will is challenged and the legal number of witnesses cannot be located, your will may be declared invalid.

The Executor

One of the most unfortunate errors associated with planning a will is choosing the wrong *executor.* A common misconception is that the executor is simply a legal requirement that anyone can satisfy. As a result, some believe the primary responsibility of settling an estate falls on the attorney. However, the reverse is true.

*O*ften your spouse is the best
selection for the position of executor.

Some of the many duties of an executor include:

- Locating the will and studying it.
- Conferring with the attorney who drew the will.
- Locating witnesses and notifying creditors.
- Locating all the decedent's property.
- Obtaining all canceled checks for the past several years.
- Authorizing appraisals for real estate.
- Evaluating leases and mortgages.
- Filing an income tax return for the deceased person.
- Filing estate tax returns.
- Preparing information for the final accounting, including all assets, income, and disbursements.
- Disbursement of estate assets as specified in the will.

Note: If a will simply specifies the assets (unnamed) are to be divided equally among the heirs, an executor has broad discretionary powers.

The selection of an executor(s) is a very important function. Select an executor with the same degree of caution you would if he or she were your own guardian.

Multiple Executors

Often your spouse is the best selection for the position of executor. In your will(s), you and your spouse would simply name each other as executor.

It's also a good idea to name an alternate executor who can take over if the spouse can't serve. This alternate could be another family member, a CPA, or an attorney who is familiar with your circumstances and assets and knows where you keep important documents.

You could also select a third alternate, such a major bank with a trust or estate department that you know could serve if all the alternates failed. Professional executors charge fees but, in return, they offer an established method of administering estates.

If you don't name an executor in your will, or if the person you choose fails to serve and you have no alternates, then the court will appoint someone to fill the position. Before you name someone as executor, be sure you talk with him or her first to ensure that the person is willing to accept all the responsibilities. It's also a good idea to stay in contact with your intended executors to verify that they're still willing and able to do the job.

Paid Executors

Compensation for the executor is another issue that needs to be considered. If you and the executor agree that he or she will serve without compensation, you can specify that in your will. You can also request that the executor serve without the usual required bond.

If you die without a will and the court appoints an executor for your estate, that individual could receive a percentage of your estate as compensation. In Georgia, for example, this percentage may be as high as 5 percent. However, the executor may choose to waive compensation if he or she desires.

No matter whom you appoint as executor, you can make his or her job easier by maintaining a detailed inventory of all your assets (see the Checklist of Important Documents at the end of this chapter). One of the executor's duties will be to locate your assets; a detailed inventory can reduce the time and trouble required to perform this service. As a result, you can save unnecessary expenses and delays in settling your estate.

INHERITANCE TAXES

As I discussed previously, your estate is potentially subject to federal and/or state taxes at your death; and, depending on how you make your will, the state where you reside, and other factors, your tax burden can be very low or very high.

Fortunately, there are ways to escape some, or even all, of the federal estate tax burden at the death of one's spouse. One of these ways is to prepare a simple will, in which the husband leaves everything to his wife and she leaves everything to him. As a result, their estates are qualified for the *unlimited marital deduction,* which means the surviving spouse won't owe a penny of estate tax when the other spouse dies.

Another provision that can be used to reduce the federal estate tax is the *unified credit.* This provision allows a person to make transfers during life or after death of up to $600,000 to people other than his or her spouse and pay no estate tax on that amount. If properly used, this is an excellent provision to use in leaving property to children, other relatives, or friends.

For people with large estates, these gifts are a means of reducing the estate's size, which reduces the assets that are potentially taxable. This can be very helpful to widows with large estates.

STATE DEATH TAXES

As I also discussed earlier, although the Federal Estate Tax Code exempts all assets left to a spouse and up to $600,000 left to other beneficiaries, the same is not necessarily true of state death taxes. Many states have adopted the same code as the federal government, but others have not. If you happen to live in one of the states that tax an inheritance, the financial shock can be severe. See the table in Chapter 8.

Paying the Tax

The amount of federal estate taxes and state death taxes can have a significant impact on heirs because the taxes must be paid *in cash.* Illiquid assets may have to be sold in order to raise enough money to pay these taxes. And due to the urgency of the situation, heirs may have to settle for less than the real value of the assets.

For that reason, it's wise to arrange for estate liquidity during your lifetime. One option for achieving this goal is life insurance, but you must plan carefully so that insurance proceeds won't increase the inheritance taxes and probate costs.

Trusts can be set up so that the insurance proceeds are owned by an irrevocable trust, thus they are not part of the decedent's estate.

What Is a Trust?

Simply stated, a trust is an entity for owning and managing assets. You create a trust, transfer assets into it, and choose a trustee to manage the assets and disburse them to beneficiaries.

A trust can be *intervivos* (during life) or *testamentary* (at death). Just as the name implies, an intervivos trust is drafted and implemented during a person's lifetime. These trusts are also referred to as *living trusts.* In contrast, a testamentary trust is set up to begin when a person dies.

A trust may also be *revocable* or *irrevocable.* If it is revocable, the *trustor* (trust maker) reserves the right to modify or even cancel the trust and to remove or substitute property as long as he or she is alive.

An irrevocable trust means exactly that; it is irrevocable and cannot be changed once established. In addition, property assigned to the trust cannot be recovered by the trustor, who is bound by the terms of his or her trust.

Generally speaking, assets held in a revocable trust are still the property of the trustor and, as such, are subject to federal and state inheritance taxes (although they would bypass probate costs). Assets held in an irrevocable trust are not part of the decedent's estate. Therefore, they are not subject to federal or state inheritance taxes. However, assets assigned to irrevocable trusts may be subject to gift taxes if they exceed the annual exemption ($10,000) or the cumulative exemption ($600,000). Also life estates held in trust and trustor beneficial interests (such as an annuity income from the assets) may be subject to tax.

Note: If you feel you need a trust to help protect your estate assets, always consult a competent estate planning attorney.

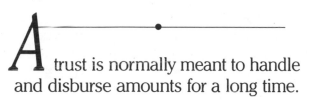

A trust is normally meant to handle and disburse amounts for a long time.

Unlike wills, living trusts are "private" documents and, as such, do not require probate. As a result, the terms of the trust won't be available for the public to read. To some people the privacy afforded by a trust justifies the cost.

OUT OF STATE PROPERTY

Another situation in which trusts can be valuable is one in which you own property outside your state of residence. This involves *ancillary jurisdiction,* which can result in separate probate proceedings—one in your own state and other proceedings in the state or states where you may have owned a vacation home or other property.

Ancillary jurisdiction can be very expensive, requiring separate attorneys in each of the states where you own property. But if all your property is in a trust, you can avoid problems with ancillary jurisdiction and also reduce the cost of transferring assets to your heirs at death.

THE TRUSTEE

Unlike the duties of an executor, which are over once the administration of the estate is settled, the *trustee's* duties can last for a much longer term. A trust is normally meant to handle and disburse assets for a long time and requires periodic accounting and tax reports. Thus, naming a trustee is somewhat more complicated and should be done only after careful evaluation of the skills and experience necessary.

Trustees can be empowered to buy and sell trust assets and transact any business necessary in the name of the trust. The powers of the trustee should be spelled out in the trust document. *Co-trustees* can be named, and it is often desirable to appoint *successor trustees.* It may be a good idea to name a professional trustee as the final successor trustee in the event that none of your other trustees is able to serve.

2503(C) TRUST

One of the most common needs for a trust is to set aside funds for your children's or grandchildren's education, and the *2503(C) Trust* (IRS Tax Code identification) is often used for this purpose. The trustor can make periodic gifts to the trust that are gift-tax free under the annual exclusion provision of the Tax Code. And when the trust beneficiaries reach college age, the trustee disburses money to cover education costs.

The advantages of the 2503(C) Trust are that the assigned assets are no longer a part of your estate, and the accumulated earnings will be taxed at a lower percentage.

I would emphasize that not planning for after-death asset distribution is poor stewardship. As best I can tell, death is not an option—it's a fact. A small amount of time and money invested now can result in a huge savings in time, money, and grief (for your loved ones) later.

You can only decide how and where your assets will be disbursed while you are living. Keep in mind Solomon's admonition: *"When there is a man who has labored with wisdom, knowledge and skill, then he gives his legacy to one who*

has not labored with them. This too is vanity and a great evil"
(Ecclesiastes 2:21).[1]

LIVING WILLS

If you have a will or trust, you probably feel assured that
your estate will be settled easily when you die. After all, you've
established guidelines to eliminate possible confusion. But instead of dying, you might possibly spend years in a hospital
bed, suspended at some point between life and death.

In the case of serious, irreversible brain damage, your
body might require the help of machines to continue functioning. These animated functions would be the only signs of life
while you were held in limbo, unaware of your surroundings
and unable to manage your affairs.

If all your estate plans were set to begin at death, your
assets also would be in limbo while doctors, relatives, and perhaps even the courts debated about removing your life-support
systems. A new federal law called the *Patient Self-Determination Act* is aimed at dealing with these situations before they
happen.

Effective December 1, 1991, the act requires all hospitals,
nursing homes, and other facilities receiving Medicaid or Medicare funds to inform adult patients of their right to complete *an
advance directive*—a legal document allowing the patient to
specify his or her choices about medical care.

One type of advance directive is the *living will,* which is
recognized in most states. It can be used to request that life-
prolonging techniques be withheld or withdrawn in the event of
a situation like that described above.

To some, this represents the right of self-determination
but to others, it is man's attempt to make a decision reserved
only for God. As would be expected, Christians and right-to-die
advocates are on opposite sides of the fence. But there is division over the issue even in the pro-life and evangelical communities.

1. Adapted from the *Financial Planning Organizer,* © 1992 Christian Financial Concepts, Inc., Gainesville, GA.

At the heart of the debate is the question of how far to go in preserving life, even if the patient has no hope of recovery. This question also has doctors taking sides. For example, one doctors' association said treatment should be continued only as long as there's a chance for improvement. Another said treatment should be continued regardless of the life-prolonging treatment. That's why it's wise to discuss the issue with your doctor before making a living will.

If you are interested in making a living will, you should contact your state health department or department on aging because requirements for living wills vary from one state to another. And if you move to another state or spend a lot of time there, it's a good idea to create a living will for that state.

When completed, your living will should name someone you trust who can speak for you and, if necessary, defend your choice of medical treatment in court. This individual is called a *proxy*, and in the same way you name alternate executors and trustees, you should name an *alternate proxy* as well.

Sign your living will before two witnesses—other than relatives or proxies—but give proxies and family members a copy of the will. Once your living will is completed, it's a good idea to initial and date it at least once a year.

As already noted, living wills can be used to request that you not be kept on life support systems. But you can also use them to ask that life support be continued.

Depending on the state in which you live, you may be able to execute a *Durable Power of Attorney for Health Care.* This is a document that allows you to appoint an agent (typically a spouse) to make health care decisions for you in the event you are not able to make those decisions yourself.

Unlike a living will, which only covers a terminal condition, the Durable Power of Attorney for Health Care covers a broad range of health care problems. It is actually required in some states as a supplement to living wills.

Even if your state doesn't have a health care power of attorney, all states will allow you to execute a *General Power of Attorney,* in which you can appoint someone to handle your business if you become incapacitated.

Regardless of what plans you make, you need to be as specific as possible. For example, you might become comatose or vegetative and unable to eat by mouth. To keep you alive, a feeding tube could be surgically inserted into your stomach. If you would not be opposed to tube feeding, you need to affirm that in your living will.

Several states already have living will statutes that say you can't refuse tube feeding. But in the opinion of many state courts, you can still reject it even if a statute says you can't. Other life-prolonging treatments that you may want to cover in your living will include respirators, kidney dialysis machines, and ventilators. Make your instructions as clear as possible. Persons who don't want to remain on life support indefinitely may place a time limit on how long they would want to continue in a comatose or vegetative state. If family members are left with this decision, it can be emotionally devastating, and there may be disagreement. That's why you need to state your desires beforehand.

Consideration of a living will brings up some difficult questions. The following are examples.

1. At what point is man usurping God's authority to determine who lives and who dies? Some would say that point is reached when life support systems are removed. But what about patients who have been kept alive for years in a vegetative state with no hope of recovery? If they would die without life support, are doctors also usurping God's authority by continuing their body functions?

2. Should families be concerned about the devastating financial impact of continuing life support for years and years? One argument for making a living will is that it saves family members from suffering through this financial nightmare. However, others argue that the value of human life does not depend on its quality or its cost.

3. If someone has suffered irreversible brain damage and has no awareness of his or her surroundings, does

this person reap any benefits from being kept alive for years in that condition?

4. Is it less humane to remove food/water tubes than to shut off a respirator or other type of life support system? As already stated, some states have laws prohibiting the removal of food/water tubes. If the patient requires no other form of life support, the only means of dying is starvation, which could take up to two weeks. The pain of hunger is a sight that has always touched Americans, as in the Ethiopian famine several years ago. But that pain would be greatly multiplied if a loved one were involved.

It is at this point that euthanasia, the most critical issue associated with living wills, arises. For example, consider the case of a patient who required no life support except food/water tubes. Because removal of the tubes would cause starvation, and death might require two weeks, some would support giving the patient a lethal injection instead.

In a 1990 survey, individuals were asked what choices they would make in the case of an unconscious terminally ill patient who had left instructions in a living will. Over 80 percent said the doctor should be allowed to remove life-support systems. However, 57 percent went as far as saying the doctor should be allowed to give the patient a lethal injection or lethal pills.

Some fear that if right-to-die measures become too lax, the result will be involuntary euthanasia, in which death is forced upon those people who are considered a "burden" to society.

As a Christian, you need to consider all the questions and issues associated with living wills. Some twenty-one million Americans die each year, and most of those deaths occur in hospitals or nursing homes, where life-prolonging techniques are often used.

Without instructions from you, doctors in these institutions and members of your family must debate this difficult issue. If for no other reason, you should state your wishes in advance.

For further information on living wills, ask your family physician or contact a hospital in your area.

* * *

I trust that you have found this book a useful and even valuable guide in helping you to make some difficult decisions about retirement. I am not naive enough to believe it is all-inclusive.

First, I don't even know all the questions about retirement, much less all the answers.

Second, space limitation forced me to make a compromise between detail and the number of topics covered. I sincerely pray that I reached the right balance for the majority of readers.

I have sacrificed several additional pages to a fairly comprehensive Appendix because there are many other materials available which focus on specific areas in much greater detail than I have.

I will leave you with this parting message from our Lord: *"Do not be anxious then, saying, 'What shall we eat?' or 'What shall we drink?' or 'With what shall we clothe ourselves?' For all these things the Gentiles eagerly seek; for your heavenly Father knows that you need all these things. But seek first His kingdom and His righteousness; and all these things shall be added to you. Therefore do not be anxious for tomorrow; for tomorrow will care for itself. Each day has enough trouble of its own"* (Matthew 6:31-34).

LOCATION OF IMPORTANT DOCUMENTS

WILLS

Will For	Dated	Attorney	Location of Will

POWER OF ATTORNEY

Power of Attorney For	Power Given To	Date	Locationn of Document

BIRTH CERTIFICATES

Certificate For	Date of Birth	Certificate Number	Location of Certificate

DEATH CERTIFICATES

Certificate For	Date of Death	Certificate Number	Location of Certificate

MARRIAGE LICENSES

License For	Date of Marriage	Certificate Number	Location of Document

DIVORCE DECREES

Divorce Decree For	Date of Divorce	Decree Number	Location of Document

SOCIAL SECURITY RECORDS

Social Security Records/Card For	Social Security No.	Date Received	Location of Document

REAL ESTATE RECORDS

Records For Property Located At	Type of Record	Dated	Location of Document

AUTOMOBILE RECORDS

Title & Registration For Vehicle	Title Number	Dated	Location of Document

LIFE INSURANCE POLICIES

Policy on Life Of	Policy Number	Company	Location of Document

BANK, SAVINGS & LOAN, OR CREDIT UNION RECORDS

Name of Institution	Type of Account	Account Numbere	Location of Document

SAFETY DEPOSIT BOXES

Box Registered In Name Of	Name of Institution	Box Number	Location of Keys

CHURCH RECORDS

Type of Record	Record For (Name)	Date of Event	Location of Document

MILITARY RECORDS

Type of Record	Record For (Name)	Date of Event	Location of Document

OTHER IMPORTANT PAPERS

Type of Record	For	Dated	Location of Document

Appendix A: Glossary

Annuity

An annuity is a contract between a person and an insurance company. The insurance company promises to pay monthly payments either immediately or at a point in the future.

There are two types of annuities: *fixed* and *variable*.

A fixed annuity earns an interest rate that may fluctuate as interest rates change.

A variable annuity allows an investment in various stock, bond, or government security funds. Monthly payments may be received, based upon the returns of the investments chosen.

All annuities are tax deferred. Penalties may be imposed if there is an early distribution.

Certificate of Deposit

A deposit account issued by savings and loan associations, banks, and credit unions.

Charitable Gift Annuity

An annuity plan offered by many charities. Essentially, money or property is exchanged for annuity payments.

Charitable Lead Trust This type of trust is similar to a charitable remainder trust except the income payments go to a designated qualified charity, and at a specified time the principle reverts back to the donor or designated non-charitable beneficiary.

Charitable Remainder Annuity Similar to a charitable remainder unitrust, except the income payments to the beneficiary are designed to be a fixed amount annually.

Charitable Remainder Unitrust A trust whereby donors can gift highly appreciated assets, such as stocks, bonds, or real estate. Beneficiaries can receive periodic payments from the trusts for life. Upon the death of the donors, all remaining proceeds will go to a qualified charitable organization.

Federal Deposit Insurance Corp (FDIC) This agency is backed by the full faith and credit of the U.S. government. It guarantees depositors of member banks coverage of up to $100,000 per account.

Federal Farm Credit These securities include obligations of the Federal Land Banks, Banks for Cooperatives, and Federal Intermediate Credit Banks. They are not guaranteed by the U.S. government and are subject to federal taxes, but not state and local taxes.

Federal Home Loan Banks (FHLB) Securities are offered in minimum denominations of $10,000, are not guaranteed by the U.S. government as Treasuries are, and are subject to federal taxes, but not state and local taxes.

Federal Home Loan Mortgage Corp (FHLMC) Securities are available in two options: *mortgage participation* certificates (PCs) are available in denominations beginning at 100,000; *guaranteed mortgage* certificates (GMCs) are also available in denominations starting at $100,000. They are not guaranteed by the U.S. government and are subject to federal, state, and local taxes.

Federal National Mortgage Assoc (FNMA)	Securities, known as "Fannie Maes," offered in two forms: *short-term discount notes* with minimum purchase at initial offering of $50,000; *debentures* are issued in book-entry only with minimum purchases of $10,000. Not guaranteed by the U.S. government and subject to federal, state, and local taxes.
Government National Mortgage Assoc (GNMA)	The most popular of the government agency securities, "Ginnie Maes" are available in denominations of $25,000, are guaranteed by the U.S. government, and are subject to federal, state, and local taxes.
Money Market Deposit Account	An account available at banks, savings and loans, and credit unions, normally paying a slightly higher rate of interest than a passbook savings account and allows an individual to write up to three checks per month. Insured by the FDIC up to $100,000.
Money Market Mutual Fund	In competition with money market deposit accounts. Offered by investment companies, they are short term in nature and invest in jumbo CDs, commercial paper, or T-bills. There is no federal insurance on these accounts.
Mutual Funds	These investment vehicles are offered by investment companies who pool many people's money to invest in securities. There are over 3,000 different mutual funds to choose from, with new ones being offered continuously.
National Credit Union Administration	An agency of the U.S. government that insures each account at member credit unions up to $100,000.
Pension Benefit Guaranty Corp (PBGC)	A corporation administered by the U.S. Department of Labor to provide an insurance program for pensioners of companies that have gone out of business.
Real Estate Investment Trust (REIT)	Similar to an investment company (Mutual Fund Company) in that investors pool their money to invest in real estate properties or mortgages.

Retirement
Plans
(Tax-Deferred)

401(k). Named after Section 401(k) of the Internal Revenue Code, a salary reduction plan whereby an employee may make tax-deferred contributions. The employer may also participate by contributing a percentage. Total contributions are limited to the lesser of 25 percent of salary or $30,000 per year. Distributions prior to age 59-1/2 may be penalized.

403(b). Also referred to as a Tax Sheltered Annuity or a TSA. Named after Section 403(b) of the Internal Revenue Code, these plans are available to employees of public school systems and religious, charitable, educational, scientific, and literary organizations. Contributions are made by salary reduction on a tax-deferred basis. Total contributions are limited to the lesser of 16-2/3 percent of salary or $9,500. Distributions prior to age 59-1/2 may be penalized.

IRA. Individual retirement accounts are available to everyone with earned income. The maximum contribution is $2,000 per year. There is also a provision for a non-working spouse, which is limited to $250 per year. IRAs for single individuals are limited to those with adjusted gross incomes of $25,000 or less; married individuals, $40,000 or less; married individuals filing separately, $10,000 or less. Distributions prior to age 59-1/2 may be penalized.

Keogh. A retirement plan for self-employed, unincorporated business owners, partners who own more than 10 percent of a partnership, and employees of either. Contributions are limited to 25 percent of earned income or 15 percent if it is a profit-sharing plan. Distributions prior to age 59-1/2 may be penalized.

SEP-IRA. Simplified Employee Pension Plans can be employer or employee funded. Eligible businesses may be incorporated or unincorporated. Total contributions, including any employee contributions, are limited to the lesser of 15 percent of net income or $30,000. Distributions prior to age 59-1/2 may be penalized.

Pension Plans. These are funded by and through the employer. Employees may be able to contribute under some circumstances. They are formal written plans that have defined rights, eligibility standards, and use predetermined formulas to calculate benefits.

Profit-Sharing Plans. Profit-sharing plans allow the employer the flexibility to contribute funds into the plan only when there are profits. Contributions are made tax deferred. Distributions prior to age 59-1/2 may be subject to a penalty.

Securities Investor Protection Corp (SIPC) A corporation established to protect investors up to $500,000 per account against the loss of securities due to failure of a broker/dealer.

U.S. Government Securities **Series EE Savings Bonds**—In face value denominations of $25 to $10,000, series EE bonds are issued at a discount and are redeemable at the face value at maturity; thus no actual interest is paid.

Series HH Savings Bonds—Sold at par and the interest is paid semi-annually. Denominations range from $500 to $10,000 and may be redeemed six months after the issue date.

Treasury Bills—T-bills are short term in nature. The maximum maturity is one year, the most common maturities are 91 and 182 days. Sold at a discount-to-face value, the minimum unit is $10,000. T-bills are direct obligations of the U.S. government.

Treasury Bonds—These have the longest maturities of the treasuries with maturities of seven to twenty-five years. Like Treasury notes, they provide direct interest and are sold in denominations of $1,000 and higher. Treasury bonds are direct obligations of the U.S. government.

Treasury Notes—Intermediate term securities ranging from one to seven years. They provide direct interest and are sold in denominations of $1,000 and higher. Treasury notes are direct obligations of the U.S. government.

Appendix B: Resources

ALTERNATE HEALTH CARE SERVICES

Brotherhood Newsletter
PO Box 832
Barberton, OH 44203
216/848-1511

The Good Samaritan
PO Box 279
Beech Grove, IN 46107

ASSET MANAGEMENT SERVICES

Ron Blue & Company
1100 John Ferry Rd Ste 600
Atlanta, GA 30342 (fee charged)
(Note: This is the firm discussed in Chapter 11 which utilizes the Frank Russell Company for maximum diversification.)

BANKS, SAVING AND LOANS, CREDIT UNION RATING SERVICES

Veribanc Inc Report
PO Box 461
Wakefield, MA 01880
617/245-8370 (fee charged)

Weiss Research Inc
PO Box 2923
West Palm Beach, FL 33402
800/289-9222 (fee charged)

BETTER BUSINESS BUREAUS

Council of Better Business Bureaus Inc
4200 Wilson Blvd
Arlington, VA 22203
703/276-0100

BUYING CLUBS

Amway Corporation
7500 Fulton St E
Ada, MI 49356-0001

Consumers' Buyline Inc
100 Sitterly Rd
Clifton Park, NY 12065

Benefits Plus
1000 Centerville Tpke
Virginia Beach, VA 23463

CAFETERIA (Sec. 125) PLAN

R J Colbert Company
PO Box 90121
Sioux Falls, SD 57105-9061
605/331-0508 (fee charged)

CREDIT BUREAUS

Equifax
PO Box 740241
Atlanta, GA 30375 (fee charged)
(Note: This group also does
background investigations.)

Trans Union Credit Information
555 W Adams
Chicago, IL 60661 (fee charged)

TRW Inc
1900 Richmond Rd
Cleveland, OH 44124-3760 (fee charged)

FEDERAL TRADE COMMISSION

Correspondence Department
Federal Trade Commission
Washington, DC 20580
(written complaints only)

Public Reference Branch
Federal Trade Commission
Washington, DC 20580
202/326-2222
(publications)

FINANCIAL NEWSLETTER RATING SERVICE

The Hulbert Guide to Financial Newsletters
Probus Publishing Company
1925 N Clybourn Ave
Chicago, IL 60614
312/868-1100 (subscription fee)

GENERAL FINANCIAL NEWSLETTERS
(All the following publications have subscription fees.)

The Cornerstone
Investment Newsletter
297 Herndon Pky Ste 301
Herndon, VA 22070

The McAlvany
Intelligence Advisor
PO Box 84904
Phoenix, AZ 85071

Financial Perspective
1600 NW 2nd Ave Ste 217
Boca Raton, FL 33432

The Money Strategy Letter
PO Box 4130
Medford, OR 97501

Good Money: The Newsletter for
Socially Concerned Citizens
Good Money Publications Inc
PO Box 363
Worcester, VT 05682

The Social Investment Forum
711 Atlantic Ave
Boston, MA 12111

Sound Mind Investing Newsletter
2337 Glen Eagle Drive
Louisville, KY 40222

INSURANCE COMPANIES (AUTO, HOME, LIFE)

American Association
of Retired Persons (AARP)
601 E St NW
Washington, DC 20049
202/434-2277

Government Employees'
Insurance Company (GEICO)
5260 Western Ave
Chevy Chase, MD 20076-0001
800/841-3000

INSURANCE COMPANY RATING SERVICES

A.M. Best Company
Ambest Rd
Oldwick, NJ 08858-9999

Moody's Investor Service Inc
99 Church St
New York, NY 10007-2787

Duff & Phelps Inc
55 E Monroe St Ste 3600
Chicago, IL 60603

Standard & Poor's Corp
25 Broadway
New York, NY 10004-1064

Weiss Research Inc
PO Box 2923
West Palm Beach, FL 33402 (fee charged)
(Note: This service normally is not available in public libraries.)

LONG TERM CARE INSURANCE UNDERWRITERS
(See your local telephone directory.)

AAL
AMEX Life
Atlantic & Pacific
Blue Cross & Blue Shield of Minnesota
CNA
CONSERV
Finger Lakes Long Term Care
First Penn-Pacific
IDS
John Hancock
Life Investors
Lincoln National
Medical Life
Penn Treaty
Prudential—AARP
Security Connecticut
Time
Travelers
United Security Assurance

MEDICARE SUPPLEMENTS

American Republic
Sixth and Keo Sts
Des Moines, IA 50334
800/247-2190

Golden Rule
712 11th St
Lawrenceville, IL 62439
800/937-4740

Gerber Life
Insurance Benefit Services
215 W Church Rd
King of Prussia, PA 19406
800/253-3074

(Note: Continental General, United American, and others are available through your local agent.)

MEMORIAL SOCIETIES

Continental Association of Funeral & Memorial Societies Inc
6900 Lost Lake Rd
Egg Harbor, WI 54209
800/458-5563
(Note: This organization will provide the telephone numbers of chapters in your locale.)

MINISTRIES PROVIDING ASSISTANCE ON
WILLS, TRUSTS, AND ANNUITY PROGRAMS

Back to the Bible Broadcast
301 S 12th St
PO Box 82808
Lincoln, NE 68501
402/474-4567

The Bible League
16801 Van Dam Rd
South Holland, IL 60473
708/331-2094

Billy Graham Evangelistic Assoc
1300 Harmon Pl
Minneapolis, MN 55403
612/338-0500

Campus Crusade for Christ
100 Sunport Lane
Orlando, FL 32809-7875
407/826-2000

Compassion International
3955 Cragwood Dr
PO Box 7000
Colorado Springs, CO 80933
719/594-9900

Focus on the Family
420 N Cascade
Colorado Springs, CO 80903-3352
719/531-3400

Friends of Israel Gospel Ministries
PO Box 908
Bellmawr, NJ 08099
609/853-5590

Joni and Friends
PO Box 3333
Agoura, CA 91301
818/707-5664

Moody Bible Institute
820 N LaSalle Blvd.
Chicago, IL 60610
312/329-4000

The Navigators
PO Box 6000
Colorado Springs, CO 80934
719/598-1212

Prison Fellowship Ministries
PO Box 17500
Washington, DC 20041-0500
202/265-4544

Wycliffe Bible Translators
19891 Beach Blvd
PO Box 2727
Huntington Beach, CA 92647
714/969-4600

World Vision International
919 W Huntington Dr
Monrovia, CA 91016
818/357-7979

MUTUAL FUND COMPANIES

American (Load)
333 S Hope St
Los Angeles, CA 90071-1447
800/421/0180

Delaware (Load)
One Commerce Sq
Philadelphia, PA 19103-1681
808/523-4640

Fidelity (No-load and Low-load)
82 Devonshire St
Boston, MA 02109-3605
800/544-8888

Franklin (Load)
777 Mariners Island Blvd
San Mateo, CA 94404-1585
800/632-2180

Janus (No-load)
PO Box 173375
Denver, CO 80217-3375
800/525-3713

Kemper (Load)
120 S LaSalle St
Chicago, IL 60603-3473
800/621-1148

Massachusetts Financial
Services (Load)
500 Boylston St
Boston, MA 02116
800/343-2829

Phoenix (Load)
101 Munson St
Greenfield, MA 01301
800/243-1574

Pioneer (Load)
60 State St
Boston, MA 02109-1975
800/225/6292

Scudder (No-load)
175 Federal St
Boston, MA 02110-1706
800/225-2470

T. Rowe Price (No-load)
100 E Pratt St
Baltimore, MD 21202
800/638-5660

Templeton (Load)
700 Central Ave
PO Box 33030
St Petersburg, FL 33733-8030
800/237-0738

Twentieth Century Investors (No-load)
4500 Main St
PO Box 419200
Kansas City, MO 64141-6200
800/345-2021

USAA (No-load)
USAA Bldg
San Antonio, TX 78288
800/531-8181

Vanguard (No-load)
Vanguard Financial Center
PO Box 2600
Valley Forge, PA 19482-2600
800/662-7447

MUTUAL FUND SERVICES
(Fees charged for all material.)

Guide to Mutual Funds (general—all types)
Investment Company Institute
1600 M St NW
Washington, DC 20036

Income and Safety (income-oriented funds)
Institute of Econometric Research
3471 N Federal Hwy
Fort Lauderdale, FL 33306

Lynch Municipal Bond Advisory Inc (tax-free fund)
PO Box 25114
Santa Fe, NM 87504

Mutual Fund Education Alliance (general—all types)
The Association of No-Load Funds
520 N Michigan Ave Ste 1632
Chicago, IL 60611

Mutual Fund Forecaster (growth mutual funds)
Institute of Econometric Research
3471 N Federal Hwy
Fort Lauderdale, FL 33306

Mutual Fund Values Newsletter (general—all types)
Morningstar Inc
53 W Jackson Blvd
Chicago, IL 60604

No-Load Fund-X (all types of No-load funds)
235 Montgomery St
San Francisco, CA 94104

Sound Mind Investing Newsletter (general—all types)
2337 Glen Eagle Drive
Louisville, KY 40222

Utility Forecaster (utility stocks and mutual funds)
1101 King St
Alexandria, VA 22314

PENSION BENEFITS

Pension Benefit Guaranty Corp
2020 K St NW
Washington, DC 20006
202/778-8800

PROGRAMS FOR OLDER PEOPLE

American Association of Homes for the Aging (AAHA)
(national organization of not-for-profit nursing homes, senior housing, continuing care retirement community, and community services for the elderly), 1129 20th St NW Ste 400, Washington, DC 20036-3489 - 202/223-5920

American Association of Retired Persons (AARP)
(members entitled to group health insurance, group travel program, investment program, discounts on pharmacy services—membership 50 and older), 601 E St NW, Washington, DC 20049 - 202/434-2277

Gray Panthers (a media watch program which monitors for demeaning and prejudicial characterizations of the elderly and the aging process), 311 S Juniper St, Philadelphia, PA 19107 - 215/545-6555

Mobility International USA
(promotes travel among the elderly and disabled by offering information on how to make traveling easier and less expensive), PO Box 3551, Eugene, OR - 503/343-1289

National Association for Home Care (NAHC)
(trade association representing home health agencies, homemaker-home health aide organizations, and hospices—to promote and protect the well-being of the nation's sick, disabled, and elderly), 579 C St NE, Washington, DC 20002 - 202/547-7424

National Citizens' Coalition for Nursing Home Reform (NCCNHR)
(made up of twelve citizen advocacy groups—to improve care and life for nursing home residents and provide information and leadership in legislation and government policy), 1424 16th St NW, Washington, DC 20036 - 202/797-0657

National Council of Senior Citizens (NCSC)
(an advocacy group dedicated to protecting the rights of senior citizens), 925 15th NW, Washington, DC 20005 - 202/347-8800

National Council on Aging (NCOA)
(individuals and organizations interested in making society more equitable for older persons—protecting their rights, making sure their needs are met), 600 Maryland Ave SW, Washington, DC 20024-202/479-1200

National Hispanic Council on Aging (NHCOA)
(promotes well-being of Hispanic elderly, working to eliminate the social, civic, and economic inequalities experienced by elders of Hispanic descent), 2713 Ontario Rd NW, Washington, DC 20009 - 202/265-1288

National Hospice Organization (NHO)
(concerned with supportive services for terminally ill people and their families to make final weeks or months of life as pain-free, dignified, and meaningful as possible), 1901 N Moore St Ste 901, Arlington, VA 22209 - 703/243-5900

National Senior Citizens Law Center (NSCLC)
(provides legal services on behalf of elderly poor clients and client groups—litigation assistance, research and consulting support, national policy representation, and on-site training manuals on legal matters), 2025 M St NW, Washington, DC 20036 - 202/887-5280

Older Women's League (OWL)
(national grassroots organization focusing exclusively on aging women), 730 11th St NW, Washington, DC 20001 - 202/783-6686

Pensions Rights Center
(seeks solutions to problems of current private and government pension systems—ultimate goal to bring about retirement income system that is economically feasible while meeting individual needs), 918 16th St NW, Washington, DC 20006 - 202/296-2776

The Salvation Army
(has special program that addresses physical, emotional, and spiritual needs of senior citizens), 120 W 14th St, New York, NY 10011 - 202/337-7200

Service Corps of Retired Executives (SCORE)
(administered by Small Business Administration; counsels individuals starting small business), 1129 20th St NW Rm 410, Washington, DC 20416 - 202/205-6762

RECOMMENDED READING

The Complete Financial Guide for Single Parents
Larry Burkett - Victor Books

Debt-Free Living
Larry Burkett - Moody Press

Encyclopedia of Investments
Jack P. Friedmon - Warren, Gorham & Lamont

One Up on Wall Street: How to Use What
You Already Know to Make Money in the Market
Peter Lynch - Simon & Schuster (hardback), Viking Penguin (paperback)

Personal Financial Planning
G. Victor Hallman & Jerry S. Rosenbloom - McGraw-Hill Book Co

The Templeton Plan: 21 Steps to
Personal Success and Real Happiness
James Ellison - Harper & Row

The Thoughtful Christian's Guide to Investing
Gary Moore - Zondervan Books

RESOURCE MATERIALS ON WILLS AND TRUSTS

A Second Start: A Widow's Guide to Financial Survival
Judith N. Brown and Christina Baldwin - Simon & Schuster

The Essential Guide to Wills, Estates, Trusts, and Death Taxes
Alex J. Soled - Scott, Foresman: Lifelong Learning Division

Family Guide to Estate Planning
Theodore E. Hughes - Scribner

Living for Today, Planning for Tomorrow
Shelly Lynch - World Wide Publications

Plan Your Estate with a Living Trust and *Nolo's Simple Will Book*
Denis Clifford - Nolo Press

Thy Will Be Done: A Guide to Wills,
Estates, and Taxation for Older People
Eugene Daly - Prometheus Books

SAVINGS BONDS

The Savings Bond Informer
PO Box 09239
Detroit, MI 48209
800/927-1901

SOCIAL SECURITY GUIDES

The Complete and Easy Guide to Social Security and Medicare
Faustin Jehle - Fraser Inc, PO Box 1507, Madison, CT 06443

What You Should Know About Your Social Security Now
The Research Institute of America Inc, 589 5th Ave, New York, NY 10017 (a free publication)

Social Insecurity
Dorcas Hardy - Villard Books, 201 E 50th St, New York, NY 10022

STOCK SERVICES
(Both publications have subscription fees.)

The Dick Davis Digest
PO Box 9547
Fort Lauderdale, FL 33310-9547

The Value Line Investment Survey
11 Third Ave
New York, NY 10017

Other Materials Available from Larry Burkett:

The Coming Economic Earthquake:
Larry Burkett predicts a crash of unprecedented magnitude before the decade is over. He then provides Bible-based insights that will help you prepare now - so that you can remain financially sound in the midst of the collapse. (More than 400,000 in print)

Debt-Free Living:
Proven strategies, coupled with God's principles of finance, give you a plan for successful money management. Burkett offers solid advice for all ages and income levels as well as examples of people who were in bondage to debt and found the way to get out of debt and remain debt free. (More than 150,000 in print)

Your Finances in Changing Times:
With more than a million copies in print, this book is a perfect introduction to basic financial management. It is a complete money guide, offering biblical concepts and practical suggestions for building a sound financial program.

Financial Planning Workbook:
Includes every worksheet you will need to set up and maintain your budget. The manual is complete with simple instructions. In addition, the *Financial Planning Organizer* is a sturdy three-ring binder complete with the *Financial Planning Workbook* and other tools to make maintaining the budget easier. (More than 375,000 in print)

Financial Planning Organizer software:
Now the *Financial Planning Workbook* is on software. On any IBM or compatible computer, you can now do the family budgeting with the ease of your computer. Not only does it help you maintain records of where you spent your money, but it gives a warning if you are overspending in a particular area. (New)

Using Your Money Wisely:
Taken from Larry's Newsletter, this book compiles concise articles covering virtually every area of finance. (More than 95,000 in print)

How to Manage Your Money:
This book is an in-depth study of God's principles for money management. It is useful for both groups and individuals. (More than 375,000 in print)

Burkett Financial Booklets:
Ten easy to read, yet thorough, booklets that relate biblical principles in the challenges and choices we all face. (More than 200,000 in print)

Financial Freedom	*Sound Investments*
Giving and Tithing	*Surviving the 90s Economy*
Insurance Plans	*Your Financial Future*
Major Purchases	*Wills and Trusts*
Personal Finances	*Financial Sampler*

Editing:
Adeline Griffith
Christian Financial Concepts
Gainesville, Georgia

Jacket Design:
Joe Ragont Studios
Rolling Meadows, Illinois

Printing and Binding:
Arcata Graphics Martinsburg
Martinsburg, West Virginia

Jacket Printing:
Phoenix Color Corporation
Long Island City, New York